LEVEL UP YOUR LAW PRACTICE

THE ULTIMATE GUIDE TO BEING A SUCCESSFUL LAWYER

JEREMY W. RICHTER

scarlet oak press

ISBN: 978-1-7336655-4-4

Library of Congress Control Number: 2020902423

Cover design by Cary Chu

www.carychu.com

Published by Scarlet Oak Press

www.scarletoakpress.com

Printed in the United States of America

CONTENTS

"We are all apprentices in a craft where no one ever becomes a master."

ERNEST HEMINGWAY

INTRODUCTION

When I was in middle school, I played a role-playing game called Crystalis on my Nintendo. As the game begins for the first time, the main character is waking up from a 100-year long nap. The overlords of the Empire Draygonia placed him under an enchantment when the world went into an apocalyptic nuclear holocaust. He emerges with a wimpy sword and some light armor. To advance, he has to kill creatures that drop coins as they perish. This allows him to buy better armor, restore his health, and purchase potions and other items that will help him along the way.

His battles with henchmen also improve his experience points. This is important because as his experience points increase so too do the power of his weapons and the amount of damage he can take in battle. All of these minor alterations better position the protagonist to take on the bosses that guard each level. Defeating a boss enables the player to level up his character in ways that aren't possible otherwise.

The nameless character in Crystalis was trying to rid the world of the evil that the Empire Draygonia embodied. He had to improve his skills, gain experience, and level up every facet of his being to do so.

Your task is no less difficult. You want to level up your law practice. The difficulty is that the henchmen you're pitted against tend to be more abstract and often more personal. Maybe you're battling complacency, doubt, overwhelm, or a lack of personal time. Maybe your opponents are insufficient business acumen, unprofitable practice areas, or a lack of vision. Or perhaps you're up against antagonistic client relationships, a shortage of clients, or a team that doesn't share your client-oriented vision.

To resolve these problems, you have to improve both yourself and your law practice. What it means to "level up" can be subjective, having different connotations to each of us. You don't need to grow in the same ways that I do. But as a matter of setting a baseline, here's what I'm talking about when I tell you it's time to level up your law practice. Leveling up means to increase your stature or performance at a particular task. It's a term that comes from video game strategy where a character in a game would achieve a particular goal to gain a skill set or accomplish a mission and move on to the next level.[1]

To help us take our law practices to the next level, I have put this book in an intentional order. Before you can get your business situated, you need to get yourself right. This starts with your mindset. How you look at the world and yourself. How you prepare to deal with problems.

Every day, you're dealing with henchmen. While these skirmishes help you gain experience points, they also take a toll on your physical and emotional health. If you don't have the tools in your pack to restore your well-being, you are going to suffer. Suffering takes many forms, and if we don't devote some time to ourselves, we won't have the capacity to focus on developing our businesses and client relationships.

Once you've put things in place to safeguard your own mental and emotional space, it's time to turn to your business. The most important thing you can do for your business is to have a vision of what you want your law practice to look like and where you want it to go. If you haven't already created a mission statement and developed goals for your practice, the time you spend thinking about and writing down those things will be invaluable to you over the next several years as you sculpt your law practice.

After you have a 10,000-foot perspective of what you want your business to look like for the long term, it's time to get into the weeds a bit to figure out what kind of shape it's in right now. What aspects of your practice are profitable? Are you handling your work in an efficient manner? Are you delegating non-billable tasks to someone else? Are you developing the kind of clients you want to work with and practice areas you want to work in?

Once you've got a handle on the business of your law practice, it is paramount that you focus on the thing that enables you to keep the doors open — clients. As much as lawyers are prone to self-aggrandizement and placing ourselves on pedestals, we need to comprehend that we are a service industry. If we don't serve our clients' needs, they can and will go elsewhere. And if we don't have any clients, we won't have much of a law practice.

It is important early in a relationship with clients to set their expectations of what it is like to work with you. You need to establish trust and have free-flowing communication. Let them know what your priorities are in handling their case. The more effectively you communicate with your clients about expected timelines, litigation expenses, and outcomes, the more likely it is that they will be content with your relationship.

Effective communication is the foundation of a functional relationship.

When you put the work in on the front end to develop a successful mindset, to have a comprehensive plan for your business, and to be intentional about your client relationships, you will be well on your way to leveling up your law practice. You won't be impervious to setbacks. But you will have developed the tools necessary to help you overcome them. You will still encounter obstacles, but you can navigate around them and maintain your bearings by having a vision and the goals to keep you on your course.

PART 1

THE SUCCESSFUL LAWYER MINDSET

IN NEED OF A MUSHROOM

Do you remember the opening scene of Super Mario Bros.? I do. Vividly. My parents gave me a Nintendo for Christmas in 1989, and I played it for the next ten years.

In case you've forgotten, it starts like this. After you select the number of players, the screen goes to black and tells you that you're entering World 1-1.

Then the gameplay screen appears. Mario is standing there on the left side of the screen. He's tiny. As you start walking to the right, you see that he's no larger than the first enemy he encounters, a goomba.

In his natural state, Mario has no protection. No defenses. No offense to speak of. The only effective measure he can take that adversely affects his opponents is to jump on them. But the pouncing is only moderately effective. It doesn't dispose of koopas, but only stuns them. It only takes one time of jumping on the toothy vines that come out of the pipes to know that Mario can't jump on all of his opponents.

Mario is one misstep away from his demise. One ill-timed jump or unobserved opponent falling from the sky will send him flying up on the screen and plummeting off of it. Hopefully, you still have some lives left. Or it's game over.

Without a healthy mindset, you are little Mario. You will encounter adverse circumstances. Your nemesis will not be a cute turtle-like creature. It will come in the way of lack of time, difficult opposing counsel, an overwhelming workload, or a critical colleague.

To contend with it, you need a layer of protection. You need to develop a mindset that gives you a fighting chance against the opposition. A temperament and disposition that enable you to cope with the "slings and arrows of outrageous fortune" and arms you against the "sea of troubles" you are certain to encounter.[1]

You need a mushroom. In the first set of blocks you encounter in World 1-1, there are two gold question marks. One delivers a coin and the other a roving fungus that doubles your size. The added size isn't the only feature. You now have a layer of protection against your enemies. Should a flying koopa succeed in attacking you, it is not game over. You are instead reduced to your prior size. You have another chance to keep going.

A healthy mindset affords you protection as well. In the first part of this book, we will look at some of the things that plague lawyers — self-limiting beliefs, comparisonitis, fear of failure and criticism, and work-life imbalance — and how we can shift our mindset to approach these things from a healthier perspective. In so doing, we protect ourselves against pervasive onslaught. But that is just the defensive benefit.

The offensive benefit is that the right mindset can propel us toward success. Not success as it may be defined for us by someone else, but success on our own terms.

1.1 CULTIVATING ABUNDANCE AND DEALING WITH LIMITATIONS

1.1.1 CULTIVATE AN ABUNDANCE MINDSET

AN ABUNDANCE MINDSET is about approaching life with openness, appreciation, and a willingness to grow. It does not change your realities. It will not keep you from failure and disappointment. But having an abundance mindset will change how you experience life's peaks and valleys.

Having an abundance mindset is foundational to the things we will discuss throughout this part of the book. If you are operating from a place of scarcity, every failure is an immovable obstacle. Everyone else's success stories are an indictment on your own situation. Each piece of critical feedback is a personal affront.

Whereas, when you choose abundance, you can accept others' successes and recognize that success is not a zero-sum game. There is no need for envy because they have not diminished your opportunities to succeed. Failures are hard. There's no getting around that. But they are also opportunities to seek new alternatives, to learn from your experiences.

Abundance thinking is having an openness to change, expressing gratitude to others, and electing to operate from the perspective that "there's always more where that came from." But I'll warn you now — abundance isn't something you choose only once. You have to continually choose it. Particularly in your dark hours. In the valleys.

It's easy to be optimistic and open-minded on the heels of success. But that is not when you're tempted to revert to scarcity. It's after failure and disappointment that you will be inclined toward resentment, small-mindedness, and fear. So be vigilant. Guard yourself against these tendencies. Choose a different path. As dark as it is in those moments of defeat, dawn is coming.

But there is a problem in the law profession of people having a scarcity mindset. This can manifest itself in many ways. Let's consider two of them: (1) focusing on the present at the expense of the future, and (2) failing to value a generous spirit. But more importantly, I want to identify how cultivating an abundance mindset instead can lead to more effective work-product, better client relationships, and a more positive outlook generally.

SCARCITY AND A DEARTH OF GENEROSITY

With a scarcity mindset, you may devolve into stinginess, pessimism, and resentfulness. A quick flip through your mental Rolodex of lawyers will be enough to tell you that a scarcity mindset plagues our profession.

One of the first articles that I ever had published was called, "The Admissibility of Post-Accident Drug and Alcohol Screens." It outlined all the steps necessary for a party to have a commercial driver's post-accident drug or alcohol screens admitted as evidence at trial. The article also discussed some of the ways those efforts could be thwarted. Another lawyer in the same line of work asked me if I wasn't concerned that I would be giving away information to my competition. I wasn't. I can't let myself think that way. I have to actively work to counteract those tendencies.

If you act as though knowledge, happiness, and trust are limited resources, your behaviors and treatment of others will evidence that. Tony Robbins has said, "You never get beyond scarcity, you have to start beyond it."[1] But not only that, you have to intentionally *stay* beyond a scarcity mindset.

Having a generous spirit will help you be happy for others when they succeed and embrace change as an avenue toward new possibilities. As Michael Hyatt has written, "Abundance thinkers believe there is always more where that came from."[2] Abundance thinking applies to every aspect of your life, from your law practice to your personal relationships. Abundant thinking will lead you to be more generous with your resources, share credit with your team, and be a service-oriented leader.

SCARCITY AND A FOCUS ON URGENCY

It is not uncommon in a given day for me to prioritize urgent tasks over important ones, like answering an email from a client as soon as I get the chime instead of drafting a motion that could affect the outcome of a case. This is a form a scarcity thinking in that I am choosing immediate benefits at the expense of future returns. This mindset is also evident when we procrastinate personally important things, such as exercising or scheduling doctor's appointments.

We attend to urgent things and choose not to make small investments in ourselves even when future benefits can be significant. Shahram Heshmat wrote, "To attend to the future requires cognitive resources, which scarcity depletes. We need cognitive resources to plan and to resist present temptations."[3]

As a practical matter, allowing a scarcity mindset to permit us to focus on seemingly urgent tasks, rather than important ones, can have detrimental effects on our law practices. We can get so consumed with the billable hour each day that we fail to monitor our client relationships and do not continue to develop business.

There are times I will be so busy doing the tasks of answering discovery, taking depositions, and the hundred other things necessary to manage my caseload that months will go by without my having done any strategic marketing.

This kind of urgency-focused work may lead to great stats in the short term. I will have loads of billable hours, and my business partners will be happy with my profitability. But it fails to keep an eye out for the future.

When you get consumed with what is immediately in front of you, you may look up and realize that it's been months since you last received a new assignment from a previously steady client. You were so busy doing the work at hand that you failed to maintain the relationship, and your client perceived your lack of communication as disinterest. The client went to another firm that would give them more personal attention, regardless of the quality of the work-product you're delivering.[4]

Prioritizing urgent tasks can also result in lack of strategic planning for your caseload. You may be so involved the day-to-day work of your cases that dispositive motion deadlines and other important dates in scheduling orders sneak up on you. You may get through party depositions and realize you've never considered where a particular case is going.

A *Harvard Business Review* article about urgency-oriented work opened with this question, "Do you get to the end of the day and feel that you've met your most pressing deadlines but haven't accomplished anything that's fundamentally impor-tant?"[5] That question not only struck a chord with me, but I had to answer it with a resounding yes.

Three days before typing these words into my first draft of the book, I was looking at my timesheet at the end of the day, and I specifically remember thinking, "I did a whole bunch of work today, but didn't really accomplish anything." I was *busy* all day and my time entries reflected that. But I was just reacting to things as they came through my inbox or across my desk. I was not doing it with a sense of purpose, and in that moment, I wasn't noticeably moving my cases forward.

There's nothing inherently wrong with having days like that. But it is problematic to allow that sort of drift to become habitual. If you are not actively planning your days and the work you undertake, the whims of others will direct your attention and priorities.

We should set aside time for strategic development of our cases and business. If you have a scarcity mindset, you may *recognize* the importance of planning but buck against implementing it because it takes non-billable time. We can combat unintentional drift and attending only to urgent work by effective calendaring and scheduling.

For me there are two levels to this: strategic planning for cases and orchestrating my daily tasks. For the first of these, I have a couple of levels of protection. I use a case management spreadsheet for my caseload that identifies the tasks I have to undertake on each of my cases from the time it's assigned to me all the way through reporting to the client following party depositions.[6] It not only identifies the tasks, but I also note the status of each task through date entries and a color coding system.

In almost every case, I issue interrogatories to another party. The cell in the spreadsheet will state when I issued the discovery requests. If the responses are pending, the cell will be colored-in yellow. If I received them, the cell will be green. And when (so often) the opposing party's responses become overdue, I will change the cell to orange. Then that orange cell will trigger other tasks I need to undertake to obtain the discovery I need.

Maintaining the spreadsheet is non-billable work, but it is essential to me to maintain the priority of handling important work that moves cases forward. My spreadsheet minimizes the likelihood of me drifting through my week reacting to what comes my way.

My second layer of safety is in making sure the dates in scheduling orders are on my calendar, with prompts well before due dates. That way, even if I neglect my checklist, my calendar pokes me in the chest and says, "Hey, dummy, your Rule 26 expert disclosure is due in two weeks."

It is natural to get overwhelmed with the number of deadlines we have to monitor and decisions we face regularly. The same article that asked the convicting question of whether I was allowing myself to drift, offers the consolation that everyone else is dealing with the same problem: "If you're struggling with prioritizing the important over the urgent, don't be too hard on yourself. The number of deadlines and decisions we face in modern life, juxtaposed with the emotionally (and cognitively) challenging nature of many important tasks, makes this struggle an almost universal one."[7]

It requires constant vigilance to battle against the scarcity mindset that our limited time means we need to respond to seemingly urgent work. We can assist ourselves by creating systems that prompt us toward active engagement in our important work. Safe guards we would have to ignore to slide into a myopic drift.

1.1.2 MINIMIZE SELF-LIMITING BELIEFS

IN THEIR SIMPLEST FORM, self-limiting beliefs are assumptions or perceptions that we have about ourselves and about how the world works. They are "self-limiting" because in some way they are holding us back from achieving what we are capable of.

The difficulty with limiting beliefs is that they tend to be sticky. Once we've formed a belief — whether political, religious, or about ourselves — we look for more evidence to support the belief and discount evidence to the contrary. While this gives us a foundation for understanding an otherwise complex and confusing world, it also means that beliefs can be tough to shed, even when they're holding us back.[1]

Limiting beliefs are self-defeating and self-fulfilling. If you believe that you aren't fit for a leadership position (even if it is something you want), you won't put yourself in a position for others to choose you for leadership roles. When you see others chosen for roles that you could have opted for, it will reinforce your belief that they're better suited for it than you. Self-limiting beliefs stunt our growth and create barriers that keep us from doing things we want to do.

Let's make this more specific to lawyering. Young lawyers know they need to engage in client development. But creating new business relationships and trying to convert those relationships to clients is difficult, uncomfortable, and fraught with perils.

To give themselves an out, young lawyers (and sometimes older lawyers) will tell themselves, "I don't have enough experience," or "I'm not cut out to be a rainmaker." And there may be situations in which those statements are true. But more often, those kinds of limiting beliefs reflect a lack of confidence or feelings of inadequacy, rather than the reality of their situation.[2] But the end-result of you relying on those limiting beliefs is that they eventually become true and serve to support your premise. You become the seventh-year associate who has no clients of his own and is unable to progress toward a partner track.

When we allow limiting beliefs to instruct our actions, and often our inactions, we create a cycle of self-fulling habits. Dr. Amy Morin writes, "Unhealthy beliefs lead to unhealthy habits. And unhealthy habits produce negative outcomes that ultimately reinforce your unhealthy beliefs. It's a vicious cycle that can be tough to break."[3]

If we want to break the cycle, we have to first identify the limiting beliefs that we are allowing to restrain us, then implement tactics that will enable us to overcome and ultimately change our beliefs. This will not be a one-time measure. It will be a process, and one that requires vigilance and manicuring. But you *can* do it, and to become the most capable version of yourself, you *must*.

1. IDENTIFYING YOUR LIMITING BELIEFS

Limiting beliefs are often deeply ingrained in us and have arisen because of some experience early in our lives. Because they are so entrenched, they operate subconsciously and can be difficult to identify. An effective way to ferret out your limiting beliefs is to look for symptoms.

When you feel fear or resistance about something, that causes you to think, "That's impossible" or "I have to ...," it could be an indicator that you have an underlying limiting belief that is triggering those reactions.[4] Are there things in your life that cause you to immediately buck and think, *I can't do that*? For some people it's public speaking. Or maybe you're a perfectionist, and that mentality stops you from doing things because you will be unable to perform them flawlessly. Or do you think you aren't smart or talented enough?

Something sparked these feelings and turned them into things that you believe about yourself. Do some digging to find the root of your limiting beliefs. You may be able to point to a singular event that catalyzed your limiting belief. Sometimes this can be painful and may require the help of a counselor. Whatever the case, if you want to move beyond it, you will have to put in the introspective work of identifying your limiting beliefs.

Only after you've identified them will you be able to overcome them. Author and entrepreneur Joanna Penn writes, "You need to identify those critical thoughts so they are not just running through your mind like black sand, squashing the life from you."[5]

2. OVERCOMING YOUR LIMITING BELIEFS

If you're going to shed yourself of your limiting beliefs, you need a plan. There is no one-time cure all. These are beliefs that you've curated over a long time. It's not enough to decide to change your beliefs. You have to replace them with new beliefs that align with an attitude of abundance and support your growth and forward progress.

Perform self-analysis. Figure out where you're getting in your own way and creating artificial barriers inhibiting your success. Then begin to remove the blockades. Do not give yourself excuses to fail. Failures will invariably happen. But don't let them occur because you're sabotaging yourself.

Give it a rest. Once you have identified your self-limiting beliefs, give them a rest. Suspend your belief that you cannot get beyond them, even for short periods of time. Rather than tell yourself that you can't do something, ask yourself how you can do the thing that you want to do but feel you can't. Rather than conceding it as being impossible, ask yourself, "How would I?" and begin problem solving. Will yourself into a better position to accomplish the thing or at least find a solution.[6]

Here is a specific example of identifying and then suspending a self-limiting belief, from leadership consultant Michael Hyatt:

> I used to think of myself as an introvert. It was the reason I didn't mingle with people at parties or even introduce myself to audience members before I spoke in public. But it suddenly dawned on me one day that this was a limiting belief. It was keeping me from having the impact I really wanted. It wasn't the way things were; it was an excuse that was keeping me from growing. So I changed my belief. I

decided that introversion was more of a *preference* rather than something innate. I could choose which behavior to exhibit -- introversion or extroversion -- based on what I wanted to achieve.[7]

Understand their purpose, question their validity. All beliefs have a purpose, and that purpose is usually connected to keeping you safe or protecting you from pain or another negative outcome. As for limiting beliefs, the purpose, while misguided, does exist, and that's why it's so powerful.[8]

After identifying the purpose of your belief and its source, question whether it is still valid. Is it true? And if so, is it immutable? Often, the answer to those questions is no. So if your limiting belief is no longer true or is changeable, then it's no longer serving its purpose. It is no longer valid. Instead, your belief is diminishing your capacity accomplish things.

Form new beliefs. To break the hold your old beliefs have, you need to replace them with new ones. We need to believe in something to make sense of the world and to give ourselves stable foundations for navigating it. "So for each of the limiting beliefs you've identified, turn it around and formulate a new belief that's more in line with your values and that'll support you in achieving your goals."[9]

We can't leave voids where the old beliefs resided, or they will try to take up residence again. We must establish new beliefs, then implement measures to affirm them.

Affirm your new beliefs. Set up habits to support the new beliefs, like deliberately putting the new belief into practice in a small way every day.[10] Do things that challenge your self-limiting beliefs. Choose goals that help you move in the direction of your overall objectives.

Your goals should be out of your comfort zone. You may not achieve them at first, but the more you work toward them, the more confidence you will build. And confidence is the enemy of limiting beliefs.[11]

We will discuss goal-setting in more detail in the next section of the book. But it's important to understand that you can implement goal-setting in myriad aspects of your life, whether it's to level up your business or to reinforce new beliefs about yourself and the things you can accomplish.

1.1.3 APPLY HEALTHY MOTIVATORS

WHAT MOTIVATES YOU? Do you even know? As recently as a couple of years ago, I didn't know what drove me. One day, while I was writing my first book and after I had pitched some great new business idea to my wife, she asked, "Why can't you *just* be a lawyer? Why do always have to have all this other stuff going on?"[1]

It was a legitimate question. One I didn't have an answer to at the time. But I do now. I was reading a book about the Enneagram, a personality type system that helps people identify which of nine base personality types best fits them. It didn't take me long to discern where I fit.

I knew as soon as I read these descriptors: ambitious, energetic, highly driven for advancement, diplomatic and poised, but may have problems with workaholism and competitiveness.[2] I was an "Achiever" (a 3 in Enneagram numerology). As I read further, the book described motivators that Achievers may experience: status-consciousness, overly concerned with their image and what others think of them, a need to distinguish themselves from others, and a desire to be affirmed and impress others.³ Even though I squirmed a bit in discomfort as I read those, I knew they also described me.

DRIVEN BY NEGATIVE MOTIVATION

We all have both healthy and unhealthy sources of motivation. Negative motivators, like spite, drive many lawyers, who carry themselves with a chip on their shoulder. My friend Bill M. Hours (pseudonym) wrote on his blog about "spite cookies." He felt slighted when a family member commented that she expected he would have eaten all the cookies she made. The comment fueled the motivation his weight loss and created a symbol for his journey: "I felt the spite rolling over me again. I decided, no, these cookies would not all be eaten. In fact, these cookies would NEVER all be eaten. I took a cookie out of the container, placed it in a little plastic sandwich baggie, and gingerly placed my prize in the freezer."⁴

Negative motivators can be unhealthy. They can drive us to accomplishment, but steal our joy. Nelson Mandela once said, "Resentment is like drinking poison and hoping it will kill your enemies."

The most vivid example to me of someone who operated with negative motivation is Kobe Bryant. Focusing on every slight and a determination to prove nay-sayers wrong drove them to great success. But at what cost? He sabotaged friendships, and alienated teammates and coaches. He was driven to succeed at all costs. And it did have a cost.

Toward the end of his career, Kobe Bryant realized that his legacy would be one not only of success, but of success laced through with surliness, scandal, and turmoil. In his last two seasons, he became more publicly engaging with the media. Spectators saw him smiling and cutting up for the first time in his career. Bryant released himself from years of negative motivation that fueled his drive for success.

We celebrate athletes and businesspeople who are tenacious and have a chip on their shoulder. But we rarely consider the toll it takes on a person to operate with that mentality for decades. The belief that what you are and what you have accomplished is insufficient. Of having to do more — always more — to prove yourself both to yourself and others. Of sacrificing personal relationships on the altar of success.

To be transparent, a fear of not leaving a mark and of being forgettable drives much of my work. And although I am not inclined to discuss my successes with others, deep inside I want people to be impressed by what I've done. I want my accomplishments to set me apart from my peers.

But this type of motivation means that no accomplishment will ever be sufficient. There will always be people who have done more. Who have done what I'm doing but more successfully. These thoughts and motivations lead to a scarcity mindset, as we discussed in the first chapter. Left to their own devices, these motivations can drive us toward a habit of comparing ourselves with others, which we will discuss in the next chapter.

There is a healthier alternative than relying solely on negative motivators. This isn't to say that we should entirely give up negative sources of motivation. They have their place. But they have to stay in check. We must prune them. Allowed to grow wild, negative motivators will develop into a thicket of resentment and bitterness that steals our joy and pushes us toward accomplishment for its own sake.

THE PLEASURE OF POSITIVE MOTIVATION

Positive motivation focuses on pleasure, rather than fear or scarcity. Positive motivation uses the carrot instead of the stick. "You can create positive motivation by either reminding yourself of the benefits of a task or by setting up rewards for yourself for completing something. It's the equivalent of setting up carrots or thinking about the carrots as you go about doing what you need to do."[5]

For example, when you set a profitability goal for the month and accomplish it, reward yourself for doing so. To follow the advice of Tom and Donna in *Parks and Recreation*: "Treat yo'self!"

In keeping with my theme of transparency, I'll tell you that I'm bad at using positive motivation. It isn't something that resonates with me. When I publish a book, I'm not interested in sitting down and cherishing the moment. I'm much more inclined to say, "Well, that's done. On to the next thing." So this section is a bit of preaching to myself to take a minute and treat myself on occasion. Just don't email me after you've read this chapter and ask if I rewarded myself after finishing this book. I probably didn't. New habits are hard to make.

As I was writing, two great examples of using positive motivation came across my Twitter feed. Former Atlanta Braves relief pitcher Eric O'Flaherty wrote about using the pleasure of exercise (rather than the guilt and grind) as a motivation to be physically healthier:

> You don't have to be miserable to get in shape, anybody that tells you otherwise is scamming you. Just walk more, eat less poop food and lift weights sometimes. If somebody tells you to do a burpee, punch them in the face.
>
> The mindset that you have to conquer the world and

have this amazing CrossFit death workout every time you go to the gym in order to get results will keep you home on your couch procrastinating.

You'll also burn yourself out thinking/working like that. You probably don't need more coffee/pre workout. You probably need a day off or some water. Or go play some d*** hacky sack, who gives a s***? Just do something. If it's enjoyable, you will keep doing it.

Don't workout so hard that you have to sit the rest of the day to recover. Go dick around in the gym for 45 min and see what happens. Get out while you feel good. If you're tired, just go for a couple long walks and drink some water.

It takes a lot of time, so play the long game, save energy for tomorrow. Just keep yourself moving. Getting/staying "in shape" is just as much about your mental well being as it is your physical appearance. Make it enjoyable and be patient ... It's going to take months, why rush?

These are things I tell myself.[6]

Meanwhile, author Joanne Harris wrote about using the pleasure of reading (versus obligation toward self-improvement or reading "literature") as a motivation for reading more: "Reading for pleasure is good for you, not because it teaches empathy (though it does); or because it improves literacy, or mental health, or articulacy, or your chance of a more rewarding job (though it does). Reading for pleasure is good for you because PLEASURE is good for you."[7]

Harris then wrote that we should cultivate that same joy of reading in our children so they will go on to read throughout their lives as well:

Some people read for pleasure alone. Some read because they appreciate fine writing. But to appreciate fine writing, you need already to have done a *lot* of reading for pleasure. If you give books to children this year, please, PLEASE give them books they will read for pleasure.

Presenting books to children as "improving" or "educational," or dismissing the books they already enjoy in favour of "the classics" is a surefire way of putting an end to their pleasure in reading, and thereby ensuring they never do improve, or read for pleasure as adults.[8]

WHAT MOTIVATES YOU?

Different motives drive each of us. Some of us are better motivated by the promise of a future reward, while others are propelled forward from fear of failure or a negative outcome. It's important to do a self-assessment to learn whether positive or negative motivators are more effective as an approach for you to use.

Whatever motivation method you use to progress toward your goals, be mindful of leaning on them too heavily. Don't let negative motivators cause you undue fear and anxiety. Don't allow positive motivators to enable gluttony or complacency. Keep yourself fueled with healthy motivation systems that contribute to you achieving your ambitions and don't steal your joy in the process.

1.1.4 AVOID COMPARISONITIS

IN CONTINUING the trend of personal transparency, I'll tell you that I am highly susceptible to comparisonitis and envy of my colleagues. I have been vulnerable to it as far back as I can remember. Long before I was self-aware of the tendency.

When my law school alma mater features the accomplishments of my peers in its newsletter without ever having done the same for me, it gnaws at me. Whenever classmates of my mine were making partner at their firms, while I felt like they hadn't achieved any more than I had, there was a pervasive sense of envy inside me. When other writers, whose content isn't particularly better than mine, sell more books or have a bigger audience, I sometimes find myself clenching my jaw and grinding my teeth.

I have told myself that their accomplishments and recognitions don't lessen the value of the things I am doing. That I need to focus on doing my work without needing external validation. But envy is a difficult thing to break ties with. It is a constant struggle for me.

Envy also runs contrary to the abundance mindset that I

want to cultivate and maintain. Success of others does not detract from my own. It does not decrease the likelihood of me accomplishing my own goals. Comparing myself to others and what they are doing does nothing but steal my joy and serve as an impediment to my focus.

WHERE DOES COMPARISONITIS COME FROM?

Comparisonitis is innate in humans. Some of us feel the pull of it more deeply than others. Each of us has our own imperfections that are intrinsic to our nature. Envy has been with us since the dawn of humanity. The earliest events in recorded history reflect envy's existence. Envy was the catalyst in the fall of Adam and Eve and the act that got them removed from the Garden of Eden.

> Now the serpent was more crafty than any of the wild animals the LORD God had made. He said to the woman, "Did God really say, 'You must not eat from any tree in the garden'?" The woman said to the serpent, "We may eat fruit from the trees in the garden, but God did say, 'You must not eat fruit from the tree that is in the middle of the garden, and you must not touch it, or you will die.' "You will not certainly die," the serpent said to the woman. "For God knows that when you eat from it your eyes will be opened, and you will be like God, knowing good and evil." When the woman saw that the fruit of the tree was good for food and pleasing to the eye, and also desirable for gaining wisdom, she took some and ate it. She also gave some to her husband, who was with her, and he ate.[1]

The serpent tempted them by comparing them with God. If only they would do this one thing, they too could be like

God. How many of us have tried some shortcut or scheme that promised to deliver immediate results? There are innumerable articles on websites that read, "Do This One Thing to ...".

We look at what others around us have done, feel inadequate about our own accomplishments, and click on the article to read about this one (illusory) action that we can adopt to propel ourselves to the next level. "When a person becomes envious, it is often due to some degree of dissatisfaction with the self. In other words, envy occurs when a person believes that having what another person has would increase their own happiness. Envy might also involve some degree of wishing that the other person did not have the envied object or quality."[2]

I am a person who, for better or worse, places much of my identity in my accomplishments. I am ambitious and internally motivated because (when I'm not keeping myself in check), I derive my self-worth from my accomplishments. So when I see others accomplishing more or receiving more recognition, there is a deep-seeded part of me that suggests that they have more value than I do or are more worthy of love or adoration because of what they have done. This in turn leads to internal discord with my own accomplishments. If allowed to go unrestrained, it can turn into me wishing others do not succeed in what they're doing, even where it has no actual bearing on me.

Like any other unhealthy tendency that tempts us, the first thing is to recognize it in ourselves. If you feel the pull of comparisonitis, learn to recognize the feeling and be aware of it, because if you know how you feel, you can control your behavior.[3]

You should recognize this characteristic in yourself so that you are aware when it tries to grab hold of you. The repercussions of submitting to comparisonitis and envy can be grave.

WHAT WILL ENVY COST YOU?

At a minimum, envy can lead to narcissism, ingratitude, and taking joy in the failures of others. Left unchecked, envy develops into anguish and bitterness that "can lead to physical health problems such as infections, cardiovascular diseases, and cancers; and mental health problems such as depression, anxiety, and insomnia. We are, quite literally, consumed by envy."[4]

We can again look at early recorded human history to see the consequences of envy. Cain murdered his brother Able because he was envious of the favor God bestowed on the sacrifice that Able had made. Cain was so consumed with the honor that Able had received for his gift that, rather than trying to improve what he was doing and had offered, Cain decided to eliminate the object of his shame.

Now, you and I aren't likely to start sabotaging our friends on Instagram who are posting pictures of their houses and extravagant vacations. We probably aren't going to kill off any of our business competition. But we might allow envy to deprive us of joy in the things we our doing. We may become consumed with others' successes in a way that derails our own ambition. The cost of envy can be great, but there is a way to deviate from the path.

ALLEVIATE THE GRIP OF COMPARISONITIS

As I was reading *Ocean at the End of the Lane* by Neil Gaiman, I caught myself thinking, *I could never write like that. He's amazing.* But here's the thing. I don't have to be Neil Gaiman. Or Erik Larson. Or Ross Guberman.

I have to be me. The only comparisons I should be making are against myself. How does my current work stand up to what I have done in the past? How can I continue to improve it and make my work product next month better than it was this month?

Rather than comparing myself against others, what I need to focus on are the qualities that make my work distinct. I need to understand and capitalize on my own strengths, and be cognizant of my weaknesses so that I can strive to improve them. You need to do likewise.

You are unique and capable of distinguishing yourself. Only you are capable of figuring out what combination of knowledge and life-experiences you can rely on to better relate to clients, more effectively communicate with jurors, or to write compelling briefs. But you will not develop those skills if you are sulking about one of your peers having a different set of skills or being a more prominent figure in the community.

If you want to alleviate the grip of comparisonitis, focus inwardly. As Jocelyn Glei writes in *Manage Your Day to Day*, "Stop looking at what other people are doing and look at what you're achieving. Stop looking sideways, look at where you're going." Develop yourself. And take actions to reach the high standards you have for yourself.

1.2 FEAR OF FAILURE AND CRITICISM

1.2.1 MANAGE YOUR FEAR OF FAILURE

WE IDENTIFY WITH OUR WORK. We often think that any workplace failure or rejection is a personal shortcoming. We spend a large percentage of time engaged in work, so criticism and failure hurt because we are so invested in what we are doing. So we have to look for ways to manage our fear of negative outcomes.

I intentionally titled this section "*Manage* Your Fear of Failure," instead of "*Overcome* Your Fear of Failure". You aren't going to eliminate fear. But you can cope with it better. You can create an actionable plan to deal with it.

FIND THE BENEFITS OF PAST FAILURES

Your negative experiences have some benefits, even if they are difficult to see or appreciate in the moment. By seeking the benefits of past failures, you may enhance your ability to identify benefits so that it is easier next time you fail.[1] Whenever we fail at something, we can choose either to wallow in it or to look for the lesson we're meant to learn. These lessons are important because they are how we grow, how we keep from making the same mistake again. "Failures stop us only if we let them."[2]

There may be a time in life when a confluence of cataclysmic events conspires against you to cause failure. At the end of it, when you're surveying the damage, you may be left wondering what you can learn from failure. And initially, the answer may well be, "I have no idea."

In 2007 I bought a small house in Warrior, Alabama. It wasn't a particularly nice house, but it was the best I could do at the time. I was tired of paying rent, so it was time to buy. Besides, in 2007, we were all still operating under the supposition that property values only ever appreciate.

I asked the advice of all the right people and received assurances that this purchase was a good decision. My now-wife and I were dating and had been for a couple of years, but at least one of us (me) wasn't quite ready to discuss our long-term future. Had I been ready to have that conversation, I expect she would have told me this wasn't a house she could envision herself living in.

So I bought the house, made some improvements, and moved in. About nine months later, we got engaged. Shortly after that, we started looking at a garden home in another town, which we ended up purchasing. That was the summer of 2008.

I put my house in Warrior up for sale, where it stayed for more than six months. The market had begun to turn. Unbeknownst to us at the time, we were at the front end of the Great Recession. Month after month, my house sat empty and for sale, with little traction.

Eventually, I listed it for rent. I found tenants fairly quickly. And just in time too. We got married in the summer of 2009, and I started law school two months later. The tenancy situation went well ... until it didn't. Several months before their contract was up, the tenants just stopped paying rent. I got promises of good intentions to get caught up, but those never materialized. They left and the house sat empty again. I tried to sell it. Nothing. I sold my motorcycle to pay the mortgage for a few months. Then I found more tenants.

The new tenants ended up staying in the house for more than four years. The bulk of that time went pretty well. But when it soured, it did so in a hurry. They abandoned the place still owing seven months back rent. They left behind most of their possessions (everything from clothes to family photos to baseball cards), including a refrigerator full of food, but with no power to it. I should have known better than to open that refrigerator door, but now I'll have forever emblazoned in my olfactory sense the odor that assaulted me. They left piles of garbage in the backyard, and a garage filled with more of the same.

Once I cleared out the trash and furniture, I was left with a rundown house that would take several thousand dollars to get back into any kind of presentable condition. But I was out of money. By this time, I had gone nine months with no cash generation from the property. We were staring financial ruin in the face. There were innumerable nights that I lay in bed after the house was quiet and prayed that a lightning strike would burn the place to the ground.

Then I got an offer to sell. But the buyer was only offering about 60% of what I had paid for it. Accepting that offer would mean taking a huge loss. A loss that I couldn't manage. Yet everyone I sought advice from said it was time to cut my losses. My folks stepped up to help me with the financial loss I was incurring. And I agreed to sell the albatross that had been saddled around my neck for the better part of seven years. I still haven't calculated the total amount of money I sunk into that house and lost. I don't think I will.

At the end of this episode, I was left wondering, "What can I learn from this?" I did all the things you're supposed to do before making a big decision. Prayed over it. Asked the advice of people with more experience and wisdom than me. Yet for years I was burdened with a house that placed considerable mental, financial, and emotional strain on me and my family. At the end, I got rid of the house, but it would be years before I could be rid of the financial aftermath. There were many days that I asked myself what I could learn from the situation and how I could avoid repeating it.

I was reminded of a scene from *Burn after Reading*, in which after a series of unforeseeable calamities, two CIA officers are reflecting on the situation. The superior officer asked his subordinate what they learned from the events that had just unfolded. The subordinate replied, "I don't know, sir." And the superior responds, "I don't f****** know either. I guess we learned not to do it again."

One my takeaways from this experience was that you can do all the things you ought to do, but sometimes stuff just goes sideways. So you just keep pushing until you get to the other side, and hopefully, learn not to do it again. Because sometimes perseverance is the lesson. These kinds of debacles take a while to dig out from. But instead of the failure being a defining occasion, try to leverage it into an inflection point. You can only do that through perseverance. Susan Peppcorn writes, "The chips aren't always going to fall where you want them to — but if you understand that reality going in, you can be prepared to wring the most value out of the experience, no matter the outcome."[3]

WHEN FAILURE OCCURS, VIEW IT AS A CHALLENGE

Viewing failure as a challenge likely requires changing our perspective about failure. And that's a difficult thing to do. To start with, we need to recognize that failure is a regular and inescapable part of our lives. Steve Jobs once said, "Sometimes when you innovate, you make mistakes. It's best to admit them quickly and get on with improving your other innovations."

We can only position ourselves to learn from failure and allow it to challenge us if we are willing to accept that failure is going to occur despite our best efforts. Morocco's former Minister of Tourism, Lahcen Haddad, writes that failure only has power over us if we allow it to: "Failure breaks only those who see it as absolute loss, as an end in itself. Failure is a wild horse you need to ride towards achievement and success. Successful entrepreneurs are experts in failure."[4]

Robert Kennedy once said, "Only those who dare to fail greatly can ever achieve greatly." On a motivational level, I want to encourage you to fail. Fail big time. Fail so that you will know you are taking risks and attempting great things.

On a more practical level, I want to give you more ideas for how to assess failure in a useful way, so that you can use it for your advantage going forward.

If you choose to view a failure as a challenge, you are more likely to think you are capable of handling it.[5] That's what we want: to look failure in the eye, assess it, and learn from it. That is the challenge. Anyone can fail. Not everyone is willing to put in the hard work of turning present failure into future success.

Conduct blame-free analysis of what went wrong. But to look at a failure analytically, you have to suspend your feelings of anger, frustration, blame, or regret. You have to ask specific question. Why did you fail? What might have produced a better outcome? Was the failure completely beyond your control? Then you can apply the answers you've discerned and your newfound insights toward your future ventures.[6]

If you set a goal but do not achieve it, set aside blaming yourself for the result so that you can discover what happened. Ask questions that lead to helpful answers, which can in turn be used to develop solutions. Were your goals realistic? If so, why didn't you meet them? Was the result due to external factors, or your own behavior? Or combination of the two? Focusing on your own behavior, what could you have done differently?[7] Ask yourself hard questions so you can improve your future results.

LOOK THE WORST-CASE SCENARIO DIRECTLY IN THE EYE

"Worst-case scenario" literally means the worst thing that could happen as a result. It is not some middlingly unpleasant thing. I have a friend who as a matter of routine says, "What's the worst that could happen?" then identifies some possible inconvenient thing. This forces me to interject, "No. The worst thing that could happen is that we have a blowout, go careening into car next to us, a fire breaks out, and we burn to death in the vehicle. That's the worst that could happen." Or something like that.

For this measure to work, you have to be truly self-effacing. Consider the worst case. Acknowledge its existence. Recognize that it is not a likely outcome (or if it is a likely outcome, you probably need a new plan). Then move on.

But don't dwell on the worst possible outcome. Visualize the positive outcomes that could result. We create the best outcomes when we balance positive thinking with visualizing the future obstacles we may encounter. Vanessa Loder recommends that you think of a situation in which you are afraid of failure, then visualize yourself running into an obstacle.[8] Write the potential obstacles down. We must shine a light on our fears to conquer them. Then look at what you've written down and assess the actual likelihood that any of those things would happen.[9]

Allow yourself to feel the fear; then see yourself moving forward. Afterward, spend some time planning how to overcome whatever obstacles may stand in your way. Finally, see yourself succeeding despite these obstacles.[10]

REDEFINE FAILURE

If you're interviewing for a job, don't view whether you get the job as the success or failure. You have no control over the outcome or what goes into the decision-making. Instead, redefine your success or failure based on things within your control, like your preparedness to answer questions.

Focus on your processes not the outcomes. If your processes fail you, you can recalibrate and develop new processes. Then try again.

But it *is* important to have clarity about what you consider failure, since failure is the object of your fear and the obstacle to your success. In the pursuit of your goals, transition from thinking about failures to thinking about differences in what you hope to achieve versus what you might achieve. "Discrepancies provide you with information that you can study, explain, and learn from so you can recalibrate your future efforts."[11]

TREAT YOURSELF KINDLY WHEN YOU EXPERIENCE FAILURE

I want to reiterate that failure is both inevitable and not necessarily a reflection on your character. So when it happens, rather than being cruel to yourself, as you have done so often in the past, choose to be kind to yourself. Try to cultivate attitudes that can stave off guilt, shame, and embarrassment. You can be kind to yourself with self-care, by seeking out a friend who will be compassionate, or by engaging in a stress-relieving activity, like exercise. Each of these choices can help you cope with intense negative emotions that tend to accompany failure.[12]

If you haven't done so before, try being kind to yourself. The period after a failure is not the time to beat yourself up. This kind of reaction can lead to feelings of inadequacy and blame-shifting, so it is important to be aware of your mental well-being and wait to criticize your actions (if the criticism is warranted) until you can rationally assess the situation.[13]

None of this is to say that you shouldn't be ambitious or accept responsibility for when things go awry. As Dr. Kristen Kneff writes, "Self-compassionate people aim just as high, but also recognize and accept that they can't always reach their goals." Rather, when your reach exceeds your grasp, take the time to evaluate the situation, learn from any mistakes you made, and plan for future endeavors.

1.2.2 BEST PRACTICES FOR HANDLING A SCREW-UP

IN SEVENTH GRADE, I was at a new school in a new town. When school started, the only person I knew in the entire middle school was my neighbor who lived a few doors down and who was also new. There was a guy in gym class who was always messing with me. Not for any particular reason that I recall. Just because I was present, I guess. Typical middle school stuff.

One day, as I was going up the bleachers, he stuck out his leg and tripped me. I fell. People laughed. I was embarrassed and I'd had enough. I pulled myself up and turned around to face him. He was already standing up, looking at me. I punched him in the stomach as hard as I could, which probably wasn't very hard. Then he punched me right in the top of the head as I hunched down to take the hit. The P.E. teacher's raised voice resonated throughout the gym.

He marched us into the hallway outside the gymnasium and instructed me to sit and wait while he took my opponent into his office. Through the closed door, I could hear the striking of the paddle against his backside. A few minutes later, he walked out gingerly and with red eyes. I heard my name called. After I entered the office, Coach Thomas said to me, "I know you didn't start it, so you're not going to get it as bad as he did."

My eyes immediately welled with tears anyway. Not because of the paddling. I'd definitely had worse. I was upset because I expected that the call home as a result of this incident would lead to a paddling of its own. So I did what most people in my situation would do. After school, I stayed mum about it and had knots in my stomach the entire night. I'm sure I didn't give more than monosyllabic answers to anything that night and that I barely ate any dinner.

The call never came. Not that night or the next. But it continued to worry me. Not enough to confess to my situation, but enough to cause anxiety about it. In fact, I didn't tell my parents about the incident until I was in college.

If I had been driven less by fear and considered the situation rationally, I would have gotten out ahead of it and told my parents what had happened. While normally, getting in trouble at school would have led to trouble at home, this was not the usual kind of trouble. I was not going to be disciplined for having defended myself. But rather than consider it this way, I allowed fear to guide my decision-making. As a result, I worried over it far longer than if I'd just fessed up in the first place.

ARE SCREW-UPS THE TIME TO COVER UP OR FESS UP?

So when years later, when I screwed up at work in preparation for trial, I took a different tactic. The screw-up wasn't outcome determinative for our case, but I definitely messed up. I had inadvertently disclosed to opposing counsel damaging evidence as part of a larger discovery production.

I realized this about 10:00pm a few days before our pretrial conference. I tossed and turned all night thinking about how to tell my partner about my screw-up. Now, it was possible that opposing counsel wouldn't discover my disclosure. It would have taken them connecting several dots to know what they had. I could have just waited things out to see how they developed.

But I didn't. First thing the next morning, I stepped into my partner's office and let him know. As it turned out, opposing counsel never realized my mistake. My partner never would have known if I hadn't self-reported. But I would have fretted over it for two weeks. And I would have known I was being disingenuous with someone I trust and who trusts me.

That is not the kind of foundation I want to build relationships on. The best practice when handling a screw-up is to own it. Take responsibility and start any necessary remediations as soon as practicable.

Walking around with a clear conscious is only one of the benefits of owning your mistakes. You demonstrate responsibility and trustworthiness. You strengthen relationships that would have been damaged otherwise. And in retrospect, the consequences of owning your mistakes are usually less severe than you had feared.

1.2.3 CRITICAL FEEDBACK OR MEAN-SPIRITED CRITICISM?

CONSTRUCTIVE CRITICISM HAS BEEN DEFINED as "a recommended set of instructions that aims to collaboratively improve the overall quality of a product or service. Often containing helpful and specific suggestions for positive change, constructive criticism is highly focused on a particular issue or set of issues, as opposed to providing general feedback on the item or organization as a whole."[1]

In other words, "a good critic knows what they are talking about but also knows their limits. They are respectful, they give examples and they judge your work by the right criteria."[2]

An associate at a mid-size firm was working with a young partner who was going through management training. They were drafting a memo for a client about a complex issue. The two lawyers had put the memo through many revisions. The associate would draft a portion, and the partner would send it back with edits. Both parties were getting exasperated because the project had taken nearly twice as long as they had budgeted for it. Finally, the young partner said to the associate, "If your writing was better, we wouldn't need ten rounds of edits."

This isn't what I mean when I talk about providing critical feedback. Maybe you've heard worse stories or experienced bizarre behaviors by other lawyers. But the point remains: meanness and bullying are not equivalent to constructive feedback.

For criticism to be effective, it must aim to achieve a positive result and be delivered by someone the recipient believes to have her best interest in mind. Cutting words neither seek a positive result nor convey to the recipient that the speaker is interested in their growth. In her book about creative collaboration, *Bandersnatch*, Diana Glyer wrote, "Having an openness and being responsive to honest criticism from those who have your best interests at heart will allow your art and your work to be the best it can be."

Notice that Glyer doesn't propose that all criticism warrants your attention, but specifically the criticism coming "from those who have your best interests at heart." These people aren't likely to offer their suggestions to cause you pain, but to cause discomfort for instigating change. Change that will improve your work, your parenting, your art, or whatever the specific area of life is being discussed.

Consider the source. Set aside the sting of pride. And respond accordingly.

COMPILE A RECOMMENDED SET OF INSTRUCTIONS

"You need to do that better" isn't instructive, constructive, or particularly useful. The constructive part of criticism involves providing instructions and information about *how* to improve, as well as *what* to improve.

For example, if you are supervising a younger lawyer who has trouble complying with deadlines, and your scope of work involves doing the same sorts of tasks for each case, create a spreadsheet or a checklist with deadlines for each item to be accomplished. This provides an objective metric against which you can measure compliance with deadlines.

AIM TO IMPROVE THE QUALITY OF SERVICE COLLABORATIVELY

Young lawyers have ambition and energy, but they need a solid foundation from which to build their practices and learn their profession. John Trimble of Lewis Wagner in Indianapolis has shared his thoughts about this with me: "Becoming a great lawyer is more than just learning law. It is about how to behave, how to think, effective writing, how to develop good billing practices and work habits, how to be responsive, how to tell the truth, how to market, how to get involved in the bar and community, and far more."

No doubt experienced lawyers have knowledge and wisdom to share with a younger generation. But the sharing isn't a one-way street.

The older generation has come to recognize that younger lawyers are enterprising and efficient. They've grown up with technology and access to information in a way that lawyers who grew up before gaming consoles were in every household have had to strap on, rather than having been immersed in it.

Tripp Watson of the Watson Law Firm in Birmingham tells this story about one of his mentors:

> This generation is unique, because it's one of the few times in history where the older generation can learn skills and techniques from the younger generation. One mentoring relationship I had was with a veteran attorney who had been practicing law while I was still playing tee-ball. (He essentially taught me how to practice law, and, for that, I will

for-ever be grateful.) However, he would routinely pick my brain about technology and how to leverage it in his own practice. I like to think that I did something to repay his kindness, but I'm under no illusion on the one-sidedness of that relationship.

Diversity is the anvil on which creative solutions are hammered out. We have so much to learn from each other. It is our differences, our varying perspectives, our myriad life experiences that make it so important for us to form intergenerational collaborative relationships.

What does that look like as a daily practice? That really depends on you. But you have to create an environment that seeks dissent and in which people are comfortable expressing contrary opinions. Some employers think that keeping everyone uncomfortable is the most effective way to get the best out of everyone. They couldn't be more wrong. An adversarial environment paralyzes people. It inhibits risk taking and growth. Rather than prodding people toward their best work, they create an insecure environment that cripples motivation and stifles innovation.

OFFER HELPFUL AND SPECIFIC SUGGESTIONS FOR POSITIVE CHANGE

There is a third component of feedback that enables it to be effective (or not). That is the delivery, which can make all the difference.

You should deliver critical feedback in a manner that will best help improve the performance of the recipient. People respond better to criticism presented in a positive way, so when possible, you should express feedback in a positive manner. To be clear, I'm not suggesting you should be disingenuous or you ought to sugar-coat your delivery. It is important that criticism be accurate, factual, and complete. But when presented, feedback is more effective when it reinforces what the recipient did right and then identifies what the recipient needs to improve going forward.[3]

FOCUS ON A SPECIFIC ISSUE

For feedback to be effective, you need to use it more like a rifle than a shotgun. Don't give the recipient seventeen things to improve simultaneously. Instead, give specific, actionable criticism in an area that you prioritize. Consider this story from New Orleans lawyer Marta-Ann Schnabel:

> I was volunteer teaching an interim practical course to 2Ls at LSU Law School, and I was startled to see young women still hesitate to present their views/argue their cases. It was all the more startling that they were very gregarious and forceful in their social interactions with their peers, including the men, but cowed when asked to make an argument in front of a "judge" or interview a client. By instinct, I pulled the women aside and pointed this out to them, suggesting that bolder behavior would serve them well. Apparently, no one had ever pointed this out to them. They wrote me a lovely note and sent me flowers.

Marta focused her critique and her students' attention on one meaningful action. Her students were then able to apply the criticism to improve and achieve a more positive result.

CURATE POSITIVE RELATIONSHIPS FOR SUPPORT

Let's go back to Diana Glyer's advice about receiving criticism "from those who have your best interests at heart." Surrounding yourself with people who care about your development and are willing to advocate for you isn't just nice because it makes you feel better. It's imperative for your sustained growth and development.

We don't always get to choose all the people we work with or for each day. But we can decide where we go for the criticism and feedback that we take to heart. We can choose where we look for wisdom and support.

For that, you may have a close group of friends outside the practice of law. You may have people within the legal community through bar associations and industry organizations. One lawyer I know went through an unexpected and turbulent shift in his law practice. He was called into a meeting with the founding partners and told he was being bought out. He was unemployed with no notice.

The first people he reached out to were friends he had curated over the years. Friendships that had formed at industry events and serving in roles together within various organizations. Friends who were spread all over the country. He knew that this group would have his back and were a core of the network that would help him find a new job.

Caris Ajuzie is the founder of a community for entrepreneurs in the fashion industry. Here's how she says her community has affected her: "The single best thing I have done to level up in my business is finding a community. I am an introvert and tried to do it all on my own in the past. This year I decided to change a few things and after getting out of my comfort zone and trying to build meaningful relationships and be a part of relevant communities, it has opened lots of doors that will be very beneficial to me in the coming months."[4]

Similarly, Joanna Penn has written about the importance of curating positive relationships within your industry. Hers involves authors, but substitute the word "lawyers" and it will fit perfectly with the message here: "You will also meet other authors at events or on forums/private groups and you don't know who that author will be in five years or twenty years. The relationships you make early in your career can stick with you for the long term and you may be able to help each other now and in the future. There will always be people ahead of you and behind you on the author journey, so help who you can and you never know what social karma will come back to you."[5]

The relationships we form are not only important because we are social creatures who thrive when we have positive, healthy relationships. But they are imperative, because when we know that we receive criticism from our advocates who have our best interests at heart, it is feedback we can rely on.

When I was in youth group as a teenager, a small group of us went on a mission trip to Monterrey, Mexico. Our first night, we stayed at a church outside the border town of Laredo, Texas. One of our leaders was speaking to us as a group. He had a tough exterior and we rarely got a glimpse of his heart. I remember only one thing he said that night: "I would go to the wall for any one of you." And he meant it. I knew from that point forward, he was someone I could rely on, someone who had my best interest at heart. That if he criticized something I had done, it was because he knew I could do better and that he expected more from me than I was delivering.

Those are the kind of relationships you need to curate. Friends who will speak truth to you. People who will go to the wall for you.

1.2.4 RESPOND APPROPRIATELY TO FEEDBACK

SOME TIME AGO, Curt Runger of Attorney Mentors sent me a text message saying that he had been seeing my posts on LinkedIn and that if I would do one thing differently, LinkedIn's algorithm would like me better and increase my visibility. I've known Curt for a couple of years and trust that when he tells me something, he knows what he's talking about. So I implemented the change.

Over the past three years, I have never had particularly good results from sharing my blog posts on LinkedIn. Usually about 140 folks see a post on LinkedIn and sometimes a few will click the link to read the article. In fact, the two blog posts I had shared before implementing Curt's changes had averaged 139 views.

I followed Curt's advice a couple of days before sharing my next article, "Don't Sacrifice Your Creativity to Your Law Practice" (which you'll read an iteration of in the next section). There was nothing particularly different about it than other things I had been sharing. But the results were different, and I can only attribute that to being open and responsive to the feedback he gave me. Within the first three days, that article was seen more than 1,300 times on LinkedIn, and the views continued to trickle in over the next few days.

In this case, the feedback I got wasn't that I was doing something poorly, but that I could be doing it more effectively with one small change. There are other times though when feedback is harder to hear and more unpleasant still to implement.

RESPONDING TO FEEDBACK THAT IS HARDER TO HEAR

I was discussing with one of my partners a case that I was handling. It was a case that had a weird damages issue. I wasn't convinced that the claimed damages arose from the incident that was the subject of the lawsuit. So I had evaluated the risk in the case as relatively small, with some possibility for greater exposure.

As my partner and I were talking and the more I described the case and the plaintiffs' claims, the worse his body language got. There were a few genuine grimaces. When I finished presenting the case, his words told me the same thing his posture and facial expressions had communicated. He evaluated the damages much differently than I had.

This left me with two choices. I could follow my first instinct and get defensive. I had been working on this case for most of two years. I knew its issues and intricacies. I knew the parties, what they had said in depositions, and what they were likely to say at trial. I had considered every angle, and I had the right perspective on this thing.

Or I could try to consider things more objectively. I had presented the case to a person who previously knew nothing about this matter, and he drew a very different conclusion about the damages issues than I had. The jury would be in that exact same position. Was it possible then (or even probable) that the jury would reach the same conclusion as did my partner? Perhaps my client and I would be best served if I elected to be appropriately responsive to feedback and re-evaluate my expectations ... which I did.

VIEW FEEDBACK THROUGH THE RIGHT LENS

The perspective with which you receive feedback makes all the difference. You can either get defensive and perceive it as an attack. And honestly, sometimes you will have to parse the phrasing of feedback from the intent to infer anything useful from it and not get bogged down in word choices. Or you can look at feedback as a chance to perform self-analysis and grow.

To give yourself the best opportunity to grow from these experiences, you should view feedback as an opportunity to learn about yourself. The opportunity is two-fold in that you can learn both from what others share with you and from how you choose to respond.[1]

Mostly, I'm talking about negative feedback. Since positive feedback is an affirmation that we are doing things well, it offers fewer opportunities to make changes and improvements. Whereas negative feedback is valuable because it enables us to monitor our performance and alerts us to important changes we should consider.[2]

Here are several ways to respond effectively to critical feedback.

Don't be in a hurry to respond. Tasha Eurich performed clinical research that found that the people who make the most dramatic improvements are those who seek out critical feedback that will be helpful. While none of these people reported that they enjoyed the criticism they received, they reframed the feedback they were receiving to utilize it for self-improvement.

The feedback seekers assessed the information they received and considered it within the context of their goals for improvement. Only after that consideration did they implement changes based on the critical feedback. "When we see the bigger picture, it helps us put feedback in its proper perspective. Then and only then should we decide how to respond."[3]

It can be tempting when someone points out a flaw for us to take immediate action to remedy it. But a more measured and considered response has a greater likelihood of yielding lasting and beneficial results.

Obtain more data. Not all criticism is created equally. When I was an associate, there was a partner who always thoroughly red-lined and altered any brief that I wrote for him. By the time he was done, the pages reflected a brutal crime scene. I could have taken from his criticism that I was a poor writer, but the reality was that he wanted me to write more in his voice, using words and phrases he would use. My work was not inherently bad; it just wasn't what he wanted. I didn't need to make wholesale changes to my writing style. I just needed to tailor it to his preferences when I wrote for him.

Eurich proposes that we should not act on feedback until we understand it: "Especially when we hear something new, it's usually a good idea to ask a few trustworthy sources whether they've noticed the same behavior. Not only does this give us more detail about what we are doing to create a certain impression, it helps us avoid overcorrecting based on one person's opinion."[4]

Before you make significant changes based on feedback you're receiving, make sure the critical words reflect a true problem or deficiency, rather than one person's preferences. Seek additional feedback from other trusted sources. Trust but verify that the feedback you're receiving warrants making changes.

Find a harbinger. Once you implement suggested changes based on feedback, you still face the challenge of others recognizing in you that the changes have occurred. Marshall Goldsmith, who coaches CEOs and other executives, has said, "It's much harder to change people's perceptions of someone's behavior than to actually change that person's behavior. That's because we tend to perceive people in ways consistent with our preexisting ideas about them, not their current behavior."[5]

To combat the lag time between the change and the perception of it, you can focus on one symbolic action that is representative of the larger changes you have incorporated. If you've been perpetually late but have changed course, you could make sure your light is on and door is open in the mornings by the time others start arriving. If you've been delivering sloppy work-product, you can start by proofreading and spell-checking your work before handing it over. These small changes can signal to others that you have modified your behavior, which causes them to perceive your alterations.

Avoid becoming a lonely martyr. Research has shown that we tend to gravitate toward those who provide us affirmation and avoid people who give us critical feedback.[6] Of course, that makes sense. One of these things is pleasant, and the other is not. So we cling to the thing that makes us feel better about ourselves, not worse. But we can be doing ourselves a disservice by responding this way. The same research also found that people tend to disengage from relationships in which they receive criticism. Research has shown that this natural reaction of dropping relationships that provide disconfirming reviews leads to decreases in performance in the successive years.[7] When we avoid uncomfortable relationships rather than seeking to grow through them, we deprive ourselves of opportunities to improve.

BEING OPEN TO FEEDBACK IS ESSENTIAL TO SUSTAINED SUCCESS

One of the hard things about business is that we typically learn more from our failures than our successes. But what if we could create a shortcut in that system and make our path less rocky? Before we get to the point of ultimate success or failure, we should create a feedback loop that puts us in a position to be introspective and evaluate our work. That invites feedback and enables us to make adjustments. By doing so, we can learn from smaller mistakes and self-correct without the necessity of experiencing some ultimate failure.

Deliberately setting about to receive and respond to feedback is a valuable tool that will help you to navigate difficult situations and elevate your law practice. Feedback is essential because it provides to you information about how others perceive you and how you might improve. Although you cannot control what types of feedback you will receive, you do control how you interpret and respond to the feedback.[8] If you are willing to seek feedback and constructive criticism, then act on it, you will create a greater likelihood of experiencing continued growth and sustained success.

1.3 PRIORITIZE TAKING CARE OF YOURSELF

1.3.1 DON'T SACRIFICE YOUR CREATIVITY TO YOUR LAW PRACTICE

IN A BUSINESS WHERE MANY FIRMS' minimum expectations for their lawyers is that their billing exceeds forty hours per week, it can be difficult to choose ourselves and take personal time. Our bodies often feel too tired to exercise. Our brains feel too mushy to be taxed with creativity. But I cannot overstate the importance of these things.

When we take time away from work to devote to family, hobbies, and exercise, we will be better lawyers. We owe it to ourselves and our communities to use all our gifts, rather than suppressing them for the sake of the billable hour. Your creative expression may take the form of cooking, writing, knitting, or singing. Whatever it is, do not forsake it.

CREATIVITY TAKES MANY FORMS

For a decade, through high school and into my early 20s, I wrote creatively and was an avid photographer. Then for a while the creative writing fell off, and I really focused on my photography. This continued through law school and into my first couple of years of practice. In 2014, my wife and I had our first kid, and the spare time I once had evaporated. There was about a two-year void where I didn't engage in any creative outlets. But in 2016, I really felt an internal push to do something.

That compulsion became my law blog. It has since grown and evolved in ways I could not have dreamed of four years ago. I have met people and done things that would not have been available to me otherwise. As an example, I had always wanted to write a book. But I never had a topic substantial enough for one. I had written articles for various journals, but most of those topics had exhausted themselves after 7,000 words or so. But after a couple of years of blogging, I had created enough content to compile a book, which became *Building a Better Law Practice*. By 2019, I had enough material for a second book, *Stop Putting Out Fires*. Now I'm onto the third with ideas for another dozen in the hopper.

I have fully adopted a creative life that I make time for along with having a busy law practice and raising a young family. In 2019 Frank Ramos, managing partner at Clarke Silvergate in Miami, posted on LinkedIn about not losing your creativity:

> Somewhere along the way, many of us lost our imaginations. Remember elementary and middle school, where we painted and drew, wrote short stories and poems? Many of us put those days and activities away years ago, and never looked back. Look back. Take a drawing or painting class, take a fiction class or improv class. Stimulating your imagination will help you view you cases in a new light and possibly lead to epiphanies for case themes or theories.
>
> Creativity takes many shapes. Here are some lawyers

whose creative ambitions have led to new and sometimes unexpected opportunities. Keith Lee has been blogging about law practice and legal tech for ten years, but his most enduring work may be LawyerSmack, the e-community he created for lawyers in 2016. Curt Runger has a thriving practice in Memphis, but he has created Attorney Mentors, a coaching business to help solos and small firm lawyers be more successful. Portia Porter writes entertaining books about her divorce and family law practice. Phillip Lewis authored a novel, *The Barrowfields*, that is a treasure.

This list could go on for a while. There are scores of lawyers who have not allowed their law practices to prevent them from engaging and maintaining their creativity. You should be among them.

Do not to neglect your creativity, whether that comes in the form of the way you practice law, side hustles, hobbies, or playing Legos with your kid. Taking the time and opportunity to recharge yourself is imperative to maintaining mental and emotional health. To do your best work, you must be your best self.

PRIORITIZE YOUR GROWTH AND DEVELOPMENT

Prioritizing yourself and your development is both difficult to commit time to and crucial. Tending to your personal creativity is not your only outlet. You also need to make sure that your creative thinking and processes wind themselves into your law practice. Crawford Ifland writes that "broad personal and professional development is vital — it's the one thing that will set us apart in a world addicted to shallow thought and work. We do this by making knowledge a priority in our lives. If we desire to thrive in a changing environment, we must continually stay ahead of the curve: continually learning, steadily growing."[1]

Along the same lines Samantha K. Williams of Aurora Publicity has said that the best thing she's done to level up her business is to give herself time to stop and think: "Making time to brainstorm crazy ideas is how to grow. We get so caught up in checking off our to-do lists that we never sit back and just think. When I'm too bogged down with an intense work week, I carve out time where I have no choice but to let my mind spin those creative wheels."[2]

Your law practice will grow best if you give yourself time to think. It is a key to thriving. You launched into this endeavor with creative energy. To continue to distinguish yourself and your practice, give yourself the time and freedom to think creatively. Carve out time to brainstorm about cases, about your practice, and about your vision for the future. Don't shame yourself for having bad ideas. Don't quash your ambitious thoughts. But do take the good ideas, write them down, and work on ways to implement them.

Sell yourself some time

Charlie Munger, the billionaire lawyer, and business partner of Warren Buffett, realized one day that he was his most important client. So he decided to sell himself an hour each day. Early each morning, he set aside time to work on construction projects and real estate deals, before working for his clients.[3] Munger advises, "Everybody should do this, be the client, and then work for other people, too, and sell yourself an hour a day."

Jay Harrington of Attorney at Work provides some analysis of Munger's practice: "Most lawyers think the path to success lies in devoting as much time as possible working for paying clients. As Munger realized, the best investment you'll ever make is investing in yourself. Set a big ambitious goal, then sell yourself an hour each day to work toward achieving it. You'll find that you're capable of more than you ever thought possible."[4]

To this end, Shane Parrish writes that it's important to think about the opportunity cost of the hour you're selling yourself. On one hand you could be checking Twitter or earning income by doing billable work. On the other, you can dedicate the time to improving yourself and your practice. In the short term, you'll receive more immediate satisfaction from your Twitter feed and billable work, but in the long term, the investment in learning something new and improving yourself carries you closer to your goals and vision for your work.[5]

This is part of the reason I take time away from my billable hours to write books and read about things that interest me. It's not easy. I'm actively taking money out of my own pocket for the hope of future returns. It's an investment, just like any monetary investment.

I write books, in part, because I want to create intellectual property that will serve as a source of income for the indefinite future. With the billable hour, I only get paid for my time once. But with books and webinars, I can get paid for my work again and again. There is no limit on the returns I can receive.

Maybe you don't want to write (which is probably wise because there are far better ways make money). Maybe you want to invest in rental properties or create a paid membership site for an underserved e-community. Or maybe you just want to maximize your ability to earn money and be profitable within your law practice.

To do any of these things, you have to set aside time for yourself. You have to become your own client and sell yourself time to grow and develop. To stay abreast of developments in your practice area and learn about new ideas and means for increasing efficiency and profitability.

You can do this through reading websites and books (like this one). By listening to podcasts and audiobooks. By taking courses and watching webinars. The specifics of how you spend the time you've sold to yourself is not as material as the act of becoming your client and increasing your knowledge and opportunities for development.

MAKE TIME IN THE MARGINS FOR YOUR CREATIVITY

I have a law practice that requires my attention for 50-60 hours a week. Outside of work, I have a wife and two young kids that I want to spend as much time with as possible. I have several writing projects going on. When people ask me how I've had time to write two books in the last two years, I could give them a cop-out answer, and say, "I don't know." But that's not the truth. The honest answer is that I make time in the margins to write. If you want to engage in the creativity we've been discussing, you will have to do the same.

Every weekday, I get up at 5:00am. Most days, I use that time to get an hour or two of work in before heading to the office. But some days, I use that time to write. On the weekends, I get up early and use that time to write or maintain my writing business in other ways. Sometimes I take short walks around the parking lot at my office to give myself time to think, and when I have ideas, I come back inside to write them down before they leave. Some days, I'll dictate into my phone while driving to a hearing. These are the margins of life in which I make time to write.

My work schedule varies from day to day. No week in my practice looks similar to those surrounding it. If writing is to be a priority for me (and it is), I have to make time in the margins to do it. Most of us don't have the luxury of blocking out large chunks of time to work on our creative endeavors. We have to create smaller blocks of time in which to operate. Then we have to endeavor to be consistent with our discipline, or at least give consistency a good go.

I almost called this subsection "Finding Time for Your Creativity," but the truth is you aren't going to *find* time. Taking the time must be an active decision. If you aren't making an affirmative choice, time will fill itself with other activities.

My choice is that some mornings, when I get up before everyone else, I'm going to work on one writing project or another. Maybe it's my law blog or one of my book projects. That decision is also up to me. But if I don't consciously choose to write, it's not going to get done. And I'll be a guy who wrote a couple of books once upon a time, rather than a writer with a catalogue of books to my credit.

Your schedule is likely different from mine. Your internal clock may set your most productive and creative hours at a different time of day. But what remains the same: if you don't intentionally make time in the margins of your life for creativity, you'll always be an aspiring [fill in the blank with your preferred activity], rather than the person doing it.

1.3.2 COPE BETTER WITH BEING OVERWHELMED

A FRIEND of mine owned a home remodeling business in the late 2000s. Although his wife also worked, he was the primary source of income for the family. As happened with millions of others in the Great Recession, his business fell on hard time. He had to start making decisions about which bills to pay for his business. One bill that he let ride a little too long was his workers' compensation insurance.

While it had lapsed, one of his workers got electrocuted and had to be hospitalized. The worker developed some kidney problems, and the hospital stay got longer. My friend's business problems had just compounded.

He paid some of the hospital bills out of his own pocket. But he didn't have income to spare. His stress levels were mounting and he was becoming overwhelmed. One night after work, he got into the shower and sobbed uncontrollably. He felt that he couldn't take care of his family anymore with his business. He was making mistakes that were leading to bigger problems. Business was slowing down. He had reached his limit. It wasn't long after this episode that he shuttered the business and went to work for someone else.

That is what being overwhelmed *can* look like. But it can take many other forms. When I get overwhelmed, I start sleeping poorly. When I close the book I'm reading and try to sleep, my mind starts racing and envisioning worst-case scenarios. And since I have a vivid imagination, worst-case is usually pretty bleak. I will wake up in the middle of the night with my mind still racing. It's a difficult cycle. I become exhausted, irritable, and impatient. Even when I'm aware of what's happening internally, I'm too overwrought to manage it well and self-correct.

We are all going to get overwhelmed at some point. What's important is that we recognize the sources and symptoms, and develop methods of coping with the overwhelm before it starts to consume us.

LEARN TO RECOGNIZE THE SYMPTOMS AND CONTRIBUTING FACTORS

Overwhelm can manifest as emotions (anxiety or irritability), thought processes (doubt and helplessness), and behaviors (lashing out, panic attacks). It can take various shapes and usually is brought on by an influx of negative emotions like anger, fear, anxiety, and guilt. When we become overwhelmed, it is often difficult for us to identify the exact sources of the stress.[1]

Many factors can contribute to being overwhelmed. Sometimes it's having too much work to do, or as in the story above about my friend, the result of not having enough work. At other times being overwhelmed is a matter of not taking time off from work. According to *Business Insider*, 42% of Americans reported not taking a single paid day off work.[2]

Studies have also shown that Americans are taking fewer vacation days now than any time in the last forty years. Not taking time off decreases productivity. In interviews performed by the U.S. Travel Association, people responded that they were afraid to take time off because they may be marked as a slacker or uncommitted to work and may be more likely to be laid off.

If you're not taking time off because you have too much to do, you are doing yourself a disservice by making yourself less productive. This in turn pushes you toward being over-whelmed and reinforces an already vicious cycle.

GET ORGANIZED

When I start to feel overwhelmed with my workload, I go to my spreadsheet that tracks all my active cases. As I update it, I make a to-do list of what I need to do with each case. Some-times that list gets to be two or three pages long. And while that can still be overwhelming, at least I know what actions I need to take rather than straining under a sense of foreboding that I've forgotten some important task or deadline.

Elyse Santilli recommends that when you devise a list of actions to take, start with a few quick and easy items first. Typi-cally, we think he need to take massive actions to institute changes that achieve noticeable results, so it goes against the traditional wisdom of prioritizing the most significant items. However, completing a few simpler tasks will give you momentum and shorten your overwhelming to-do list. You will feel the progress you're making and get back into the flow of acting.[3]

Another important aspect of reining things back in is to cull or postpone anything that doesn't really need doing. If some-thing can be put off for a couple of weeks with no repercussions, calendar it out to do later. Assign things to others to handle. Or if the task is unimportant cull it from the list until you have the capacity to handle it. "Most of us are prone to over-engineering solutions to problems. What really needs to be done? What tasks overcomplicate the matter or don't add value? What can you postpone for a few weeks? You should be able to cross out a good chunk of your to-do list by answering these questions."[4]

DELEGATE TO YOUR TEAM

When you have an abundance of work or pressing deadlines, it is important to rely on family, colleagues, and your support staff to help you weather the storm. You can't handle all your priorities by yourself. You will have to outsource some things or face being in a perpetual tizzy. You'll be like the Tasmanian Devil spinning from one obligation to the next, leaving in your wake a path of destruction.

Sometimes it's a matter of pride that keeps us from asking for help. For others, it's a matter of not asking because we don't want to burden those around us. But if we have cultivated positive relationships and surrounded ourselves with a supportive community, we will have people willing and able to provide assistance when we decide to ask.

TAKE BREAKS TO RECHARGE

When you're overwhelmed, the last thing you feel like doing is taking a break. But walking away from things, even for ten or fifteen minutes, can allow you to recharge and refocus.

As I mentioned in the last section, when the weather cooperates, I try to take a couple of short walks during the workday. I work at an office park, so this means that all I have to walk around is a large asphalt parking lot. There is a tree line along the far end of the parking lot with a nest of honeybees that's taken up residence in one of the trees, so those distract from the otherwise monotonous view of vehicles. When I'm on these walks, I disallow myself from looking at my phone. And I try not to think about what I've been working on or what I need to be working on.

These walks give me a few minutes to disengage, so I try to remain true to that. Friedrich Nietzsche once wrote, "All truly great thoughts are conceived while walking." So I step away for ten minutes or so, and try to tap into that. To give my brain a reprieve from consciously problem-solving, and allow things to percolate under the surface. I've often found that afterward, I can more clearly word the argument I've been working on or that I have a renewed energy for the tasks that demand my attention. Psychiatrist Judith Orloff suggests that to survive these potentially oppressive busy stretches, you should plan mini-breaks which can be as subtle as, for just a minute, taking a few deep breaths and trying to reestablish some clarity and focus.[5]

Being overwhelmed is a condition that sometimes tells us we have allowed ourselves to take on too much and our stress levels have breached the point of being bearable. Sometimes being overwhelmed is temporary because of the way things fall on the calendar. But if you find that the problem is more perennial, it is time so assess the source and make some adjustments.

1.3.3 MAINTAIN A FUNCTIONAL WORK-LIFE IMBALANCE

THERE IS NO WORK-LIFE BALANCE – there is only an imbalance that you must manage. I felt like that was important to say up front. There are hundreds of articles about achieving work-life balance, I firmly believe they're mostly ... hogwash.

We need to release ourselves from the pressure of believing there is a balance to achieve among work, family, and our other competing obligations. When we are working or commuting ten or eleven hours a day, then we only see our families for about four waking hours. If you have young kids, you may see them less than that.

This is inherently imbalanced. But it is possible to maintain a functional work-life imbalance by establishing priorities, then setting boundaries and guarding them.

One of my priorities is to leave the office by 5:00pm every day so that I can be home to have dinner with my family, do bath time with the kids, and play (which mostly devolves into wrestling) before bedtime. To achieve this and meet my billable goals for myself, I get up at 5:00am every morning. This enables me to have an hour or more of billable entries in the books before I get into the office. When necessary, I'll do the same on the weekends — get up before the rest of the house and get some billable work in (although we've already established that my preference is to spend this time on creative work).

While that is the goal, there are times that I am unable to maintain it. With a litigation practice, the days can get long in the weeks before and during trial.

Entrepreneur Linsey Knerl addresses the issue this way:

> While occasional streaks of working at a maddening pace are sometimes needed ... it shouldn't be your new normal. Celebrity entrepreneurs, like Elon Musk, claim that 80-hour workweeks are where it's at, but many thriving and successful startup founders say otherwise. The only place frantic, reckless work schedules will get you is in the hospital. Your company needs you. Your customers need you. Don't put your health at risk in the name of working harder.[1]

Consistently working 12-hour days is not a functional imbalance. It is an unsustainable imbalance, particularly if you have familial or other obligations on your time.

Chronic overworking leads to burnout and causes you to work at less than your optimum quality output levels. Over-working is like running up a steep hill. You can do it for a while, but after time, you may still be keeping your running form but the progress you're making is diminished.

Take time to assess your own limits. Honestly, I'm usually picking at the outer thresholds of my limits. The final quarter of 2019 is a good example of this. In October, I billed 235 hours preparing for two trials and managing everything else that was going on. I recall telling one of my partners that I wasn't having fun anymore, and knowing that pace wasn't sustainable for me. I also wrote 5,800 words toward this and other writing projects.

I reined it back in for November with about 150 hours and billed little during the Thanksgiving holiday. I also wrote more than 12,000 words that month. December saw both the word count and billable hours tick back up. But I pushed myself hard during the first two-thirds of the month so that I could take several days "off" (meaning not being in the office and reducing my time entries to a couple of hours a day) around the holidays.

It's relatively easy in this profession to be guilted into working beyond your capacity. That's been the culture for as far back as anyone can remember. I was at a conference with a group of managing partners recently when one person complained that her younger lawyers didn't want to bill 2,200 hours a year like she was accustomed to.

Of course, no one really *wants* to bill 2,200 hours a year. Law firm culture has conditioned us to expect it from ourselves and others. But it is time to deviate from unsustainable practices and implement work schedules that, while still imbalanced, are functional and enable us to maintain our mental, emotional, and physical health.

Pharmacist and health coach, Angela Doucette says that when she committed to self-care, she saw improvements with stronger client relationships and a more effective business: "When I started giving my body and mind the time and energy it needed, I was showing up 100% and being fully present with my clients. The results were stronger relationships and a powerfully run business."[2] Those are the key to a successful law practice as well — sustainable business practices and strong client relationships. So we should begin by implementing measures that put in a position — physically, mentally, and emotionally — to achieve these objectives. That limit the likelihood of us being overwhelmed and that keep our inherent imbalance functional.

If you choose to indefinitely overwork yourself, you will reach a breaking point. There will be burnout. You'll become uninterested in your work and your business. "The ideas that once empowered you to go full-throttle for 18 hours a day will become routine and boring. You'll go through the motions of being a business owner without excitement or passion. If this happens, wake up!"[3]

If you have already begun to experience these symptoms, it's time to make a change — actually, it was time to make a change a while ago, but now is your opportunity to course correct. When we are overwhelmed at work, we can lose sight of our priorities. We have values and interests competing for our time, and it's not hard to let them get out of alignment.

Writer and life coach Elyse Santilli puts it this way: "You can do anything, but not everything. When you have multiple passions, it's hard to accept that you can't always juggle work, personal and creative projects, extra education, housework, friendships, errands, meeting with the accountant and electrician, 'me' time, dance class, book club and write that novel all at once."[4]

You will have to make choices about what activities are doable at certain cycles of life. I was an avid runner from for about five years from about 2010 to 2015. Then we had first one kid and later a second. I started blogging and writing books. I couldn't sustain all the activities I wanted to do. So for now, I've decided to let go of distance running. I still miss it. One day I'll pick it back up again. But at this stage of life, I wasn't able to maintain a functional work-life *im*balance that included distance running.

Chris Myers, the CEO of Yellow Express, uses an illustration of our time commitments being made of either glass or rubber balls:

> In life, we're forced to juggle, and some of the balls are made of glass and shatter when dropped while others are made of rubber and always bounce back. When juggling priorities, it's important to remember that matters of the heart, be they relationships, family, or personal fulfillment, are made of glass. If you drop them, they're irreparably damaged. Work, on the other hand, is rubber. Even when you make a terrible mistake and drop the ball, it always bounces back. The key to happiness is recognizing which ball is which.
>
> For me, priorities are absolute and fall into three categories. My first priorities are the needs of family. That ball is made of glass, and I do my best to protect it. My second priority is my company. For entrepreneurs and leaders, work needs to be a higher priority than it is for most people. The reason for this is that it isn't just about dealing with your job. As the leader of a company, you have many people who depend on you, including team, clients, and investors. The third priority is personal fulfillment. If you've taken care of your family and your team, then you have the right to focus on yourself. Clearly defining these priorities makes dealing with even the most overwhelming of situations more manageable.[5]

If you haven't consciously ranked the competing obligations for your time and assessed whether you are properly tending to them in their respective orders, it's time to do so. Like mine, your days are likely imbalanced with the bulk of your waking hours being spent working.

But if you create and maintain an imbalance that enables you to tend and cultivate your other obligations, the imbalance will remain functional. You will be able to flourish and sustain the imbalance indefinitely.

PART 2

KNOW AND HANDLE YOUR BUSINESS

I HAVE FIREBALLS!

Alright, I don't have a specific recollection of shouting, "I have fireballs!" the first time that I encountered a fire flower in Super Mario Bros. But it seems reasonable to conclude that I probably did. Getting fireballs was revelatory in the game.

Come to think of it, having fireballs would be a revelation in most any world. There are plenty of times when I would have gladly incinerated opposing counsel or (dare I say it) a judge with a tidy ball of flame. But that's not where we're headed with this analogy.

When you get ahold of your business, you get fireballs. There are lots of good lawyers in the world. And there are plenty of good businesspeople. But there is a deficit of lawyers who are also good businesspeople. The problem lies in that there are too many lawyers who conflate the two things.

They envision themselves as good lawyers and believe that skill consequently makes them good businesspeople. They reach this conclusion with no evidence to support it, and sometimes with evidence suggesting that they should draw a contrary inference.

Fireballs let you go on the offensive. Fireballs are your comprehension of the business of practicing law. Developing a vision and goals for your practice forces you to implement strategies and tactics to achieve them. Understanding your business means you are able to stop reacting defensively.

Along with your vision, you will establish key performance indicators to monitor your progress. You will create opportunities for yourself where they did not exist before. You will focus on processes that drive you toward success. And you will minimize distractions and inefficiencies.

All of this will be possible because you have fireballs. You have an offensive weapon. You understand your business, you know where you want to go, and you are putting measures in place to get there.

This part of the book is about giving you the tools to do that. Look at these chapters as fire flowers. There are gobs of koopas and goombas out there. Let's get ready to torch them.

2.1 DEVELOP A VISION FOR YOUR LAW PRACTICE

2.1.1 DEVELOP A VISION FOR YOUR LAW PRACTICE

I AM NEAR-SIGHTED, which is really only useful for tying knots with fishing line or doing anything else that I can do within 18 inches of my face. I didn't always know I was near-sighted. It wasn't until I started driving that I discovered it. My mother was riding with me while I had my learner's permit when she abruptly turned to me and asked, "Why didn't you stop at that stop sign?"

I replied earnestly, "What stop sign?"

She immediately decided and announced, "We are going to make you an eye appointment."

It wasn't until I walked out of that eye appointment, now wearing glasses, that I discovered what I had been missing. I distinctly remember noticing that the leaves on distant trees had edges, rather than just being a green, roundish mass. My vision wasn't so bad that it was debilitating, unless you consider missing traffic signals to be debilitating, but it was limiting me in ways that I hadn't appreciated.

HAVE A VISION FOR YOUR LAW PRACTICE

When we don't have a vision for our law practices, we are limiting ourselves in ways that we may not appreciate. There are times we get so busy with our cases that we neglect marketing and developing relationships. We are so driven by the work at hand that we fail to set goals, act to achieve our goals, or otherwise map out our futures.

Even at our busiest, we must make sure we are actively progressing toward having the practice we envision for ourselves. We cannot afford to allow our business to coast for prolonged periods. The time and energy lost in course-correcting is more costly than the effort that goes into forging ahead on your intended path.

DOES YOUR FIRM HAVE A VISION OR MISSION STATEMENT?

One of the best ways to develop a vision for your law practice is to take the time to think through and write down a mission or vision statement for your firm. There are five steps for developing a vision statement for your law practice.

- **Identify your ideal client**

Sit down and figure out who you want to serve. Who is the ideal person or entity that you want to represent? You can do this by understanding what your practice is and what it is not. While this exercise will not be an explicit part of your vision statement, it is imperative that, to write an effective vision statement, you are self-effacing about your client's identity.

- **Define what your firm does for its clients**

Your clients need to know that you understand their problems and why you are the right choice for them. This part of your mission statement should be specific, rather than a generic claim that you want to seek justice for people. For example, here is a part of my firm bio that serves as a mission statement: "My priority is to collaborate with clients to achieve efficient and effective results by way of tenacious advocacy. I strive to align my tactics and objectives with my client's goals in handling cases."

Melissa Hall of Smol Law in Seattle describes herself as a "primary care lawyer" and identifies her services like this: "Making 'let me talk to my attorney' a reality for people who have mostly seen it as a joke."[1]

In his mission statement, Tripp Watson of The Watson Firm addresses how he will add value for clients: "Our firm's mission is to provide new and veteran entrepreneurs the advice and service that allows them to focus on building their business, without having to worry about the details of legal compliance, liabilities, or other distractions. Further, we strive to add value to our clients' businesses by providing legal and business advice that contributes to the bottom line."[2]

- **Define what your firm does for its employees**

Of the three components of a mission statement, I suspect that what the firm does for its employees is often the most overlooked. We know it's important to identify and meet our clients' needs, and we are certainly going to look out for ourselves (part 3). But what about the associates, staff, and paraprofessionals who play such an integral role in the success, productivity, and profitability of our law practices?

This section of your mission statement should set out what

qualities are important for your firm's employees to have and what kind of environment you want to cultivate. You may want to emphasize things like fairness, respect for ideas, creative problem-solving, or empowerment. In short, this should tell your employees what are the important attributes your firm wants to foster. It is equally important that your actions and mindset support the statement.

Your team needs to understand your vision so they have confidence in your processes. Arne Giske of the Millennial Entrepreneur Podcast says that trusting her team has been vital to her success because she has defined her goals with her team, allowing them to operate more smoothly. Giske wrote, "I'd say the secret sauce that has allowed me to level up my business recently is having full trust in my team's abilities to deliver."[3]

- **Establish what your firm does for its partners**

What do you want from your practice — profitability, growth, peace of mind? Is it important to you that your personal relationships are rich or rewarding? Do you want to have partners with a particular mentality? Your mission statement should set out (again with specificity) what you want from and for your business, stated in terms concrete enough for you to take affirmative actions to achieve them.

- **Analyze and revise your vision statement**

If I've learned anything from writing consistently over the past four years, it's that you never get it exactly right on the first draft. In fact, most first drafts are poor representations of what you want to say. The importance of your first draft is that you've written everything down so that you can prune, shear, and spruce the contents as needed.

Your vision statement is no different. This document will not only memorialize your vision for your practice, but will also enable you to provide the specificity to execute the vision for sustained success. Take the time to ensure that it reflects your true values and communicates your message effectively.

Remember that being a good lawyer does not mean you are necessarily a good business person. You have to practice being good at business just like you practice improving your lawyering craft. Having a vision for your practice is an important part of being a thriving lawyer and business person.

BE A HUNTER, NOT A SCAVENGER

Tyrannosaurus Rex looks like a fierce predator. He is a universal favorite among children as their favorite dinosaur. But it turns out that T-Rex likely had bad eyesight and definitely had scrawny arms. Scientists have discerned that his poor vision and limited reach possibly relegated him to being a scavenger. He may not be the apex predator that we have long imagined him to be. He just looks like one. The reptilian equivalent of a coyote.

Don't put yourself in the position of picking over the leavings of others. Have a vision for the direction of your law practice. Have the tenacity to execute your vision. Make opportunities for yourself by knowing what you want and having the audacity to achieve it.

Having a vision for your practice may not make you impervious to a catastrophic meteor strike, but it will give you the tools to identify who you want to serve, how to market to them, and how to identify their problems. It will enable you to set goals that align with your mission. And it will help you plan for the future success of your firm, rather than being limited to what is within eighteen inches of your face.

2.1.2 FOCUS ON PROCESSES, NOT OUTCOMES

IN A RADIO INTERVIEW on The Paul Finebaum Show in May 2019, Nick Saban was talking about the importance of focusing on processes instead of results: "I think at some point in time or when you start thinking about outcomes ... outcomes can be a distraction. Whether you want to win awards for yourself or you just want to win a championship for your team. And I don't think there's anything wrong with either one of those things, but when you start focusing on outcomes, it's sort of a distraction, because you really need to focus on what you need to do to get the outcome."

Past outcomes are not indicative of future results unless they are built on a foundation of trustworthy processes. Approach each day with systems in place to give yourself the greatest likelihood of success. (1) Put processes in place to manage your cases and practice. Spreadsheets work really well for me, but you have to do what works for you. (2) Be consistent in implementing and working with your processes. (3) After time, evaluate your results (whether that's how a case ultimately resolved or just that you're regularly getting discovery in/out promptly) to evaluate whether your processes are working for you. (4) Modify your processes as needed. (5) Persist.

DON'T BE MISLED BY FOCUSING ON RESULTS

My basement was kind of a disaster. Boxes haphazardly strewn about. Tools and equipment that I had not organized in the last twenty months, despite the best of intentions. Kids' toys that they had played with and discarded. A pile of things to take to the landfill. So after months of trying not to notice the mess, I picked up and organized the basement. Now I have a tidy basement.

But if I just focus on the result that now I have a clean and well-organized basement, I will turn around in a few months to discover it has devolved to its chaotic state again. Right now, I am a guy who just has a tidy basement in this moment. I haven't put the processes in place to be the kind of guy who keeps his basement in good shape.

Focusing on the results instead of the processes can be misleading. You can manufacture a good result or have the good fortune to luck into a positive outcome. But if you don't install the systems and habits which allow for consistency, no particular outcome will reveal the true state of affairs or enable consistency over time.

What are your processes for handling clients? For managing cases? For attending to your practice? Put systems in place to ensure that you are being consistent month after month. This consistency will enable you to audit your processes to see if there are any gaps or if you need to tinker with something.

If you've been reading my work for any length of time, you know that spreadsheets are how I keep myself organized and stay on top of my caseload. When I go a few weeks (or dare I admit, months) without updating the spreadsheets that reflect the status of my cases or upcoming trial settings, I feel disorganized and a little fraught that something may fall through the cracks. The other problem with failing to keep up with my processes (aside from increased anxiety levels) is how long it takes to catch up. It is far easier and more efficient to keep up rather than catch up. Once your processes are in place, implement them. Otherwise, they're not your processes; they're just a way that you spent a few hours organizing some information that one time.

PROCESSES DRIVE CONSISTENCY

If you want to sustain a successful practice that spans decades, you need consistent results. Nothing can deliver consistent results like maintaining the processes that got you there in the first place.

In discussing the upcoming 2018 season, New England Patriots head coach Bill Belichick reportedly said, "We've just got to keep stringing days together. Take advantage of our opportunities to go out there and improve and trust the process."[1]

That's what you and I have to do — string days together in which we are implementing the processes we've put in place and evaluating them for the possibility of improvement. Sam Hinkie, former general manager of the Philadelphia 76ers, said this on his first day on the job in 2013: "We talk a lot about process — not outcome — and trying to consistently take all the best information you can and consistently make good decisions. Sometimes they work and sometimes they don't, but you reevaluate them all."[2] Seven years later, although he's no longer with the team, the processes he put in place have put the 76ers on the cusp of great success.

Entrepreneur Lizzie Davey recommends that we do one thing, however small it maybe, every day to move our businesses forward. Maybe it's as simple as updating your firm's social media sites or soliciting a review from a client. Davey contends, "If you're consistently performing one task every day with the future of your business in mind, you'll be moving your business forward 30 steps each month."[3]

Marketing, caseload management, meeting your billable goals — whatever area of your practice you consider, there are systems you can develop to help you deliver consistent results over time. No individual result will be indicative of whether your systems are working. Only a long-term vision and observation of your results provide you with the information to assess whether your processes are effective or need revision.

But if you don't have processes and you're just flitting from one trendy method of doing things to another, you can never expect consistency. You won't know what is or is not working, because you will not have allowed yourself to have enough information to evaluate the source of your successes or failures before moving on to the next thing.

Being process oriented, rather than results driven, will lead to consistent outcomes over time. So just have some sticktoitiveness about yourself, and keep improving your craft.[4]

2.1.3 DEFINE WHAT SUCCESS
MEANS FOR YOU

WHY ARE YOU PRACTICING LAW? What is it that you want for yourself or your clients? If your answer is some variation of "Make money and help people," you may need to dig a little deeper. Lawyers are not a homogeneous group. We all strive for different things, for different reasons. What is true for you today may change over time; it has for me. All the same, it is important to identify your motivations so you can measure your journey, celebrate your successes, and understand how far you've come over time.[1]

Earlier in the book, we discussed billionaire lawyer Charlie Munger's habit of selling himself an hour each day before working for his clients. A practice that eventually led to immense wealth. Part of the reason he was able to sustain that practice is that he knew what success meant to him: "I had a considerable passion to get rich. Not because I wanted Ferraris – I wanted the independence. I desperately wanted it. I thought it was undignified to have to send invoices to other people. I don't where I got that notion from, but I had it." Success for him was financial independence.

I can't define what success means for you. I can barely define what it means for me. It can be difficult to get past the superficial evidence of successes and get to the root of our ambitions. And once you've done it, you have to keep doing it. What defines success for you is not static. It is not immutable.

But there are questions you can ask of yourself that may aid you in defining success as it pertains to your legal career and professional endeavors: (1) What is your definition of success for your law practice? (2) How will you track and measure that success? (3) What do you want to do with that success? (4) What is the point in your legal work?

Note that I do not intend the last question to be rhetorical or sarcastic, although there are plenty of days that your clients will cause a genuine question of "What's the point?" to be sardonic.

At this point I want to provide you some examples and motivations of how other people have found fulfillment in their work that matched their definition of success.

Let's start with iconic UCLA basketball coach John Wooden: "Success is peace of mind, which is a direct result of self-satisfaction in knowing you did your best to become the best you are capable of becoming."

Ron Cordes, founder of the Cordes Foundation, which advocates for entrepreneurship and economic opportunities for women, had this definition: "To find and fully live your purpose in life, and to leave an enduring legacy of having made a difference in the world."

Raj Sisodia, co-founder of Conscious Capitalism and professor at Babson College: "I define success as living my true purpose and having a positive impact on the lives of people by uplifting them and inspiring them to think and act in ways that they may not have considered before."

Jeremy Young, CEO of the lifestyle retail outlet Tanga:

"Success, for me, has always been in providing a great quality of life for my family, for those who work for me, and to my community."

Dan Kurzius, co-founder and COO of Mailchimp: "To me, success means creating a business that empowers customers, employees, and community in equal measure. We want to add positive value to people's lives, from a personal and professional standpoint."

Winston Churchill, whose sentiments I can identify with more readily than I'd like: "Success is going from failure to failure without losing enthusiasm."

Finally, Stephen Covey, author of *The Seven Habits of Highly Effective People*: "If you carefully consider what you want to be said of you in the funeral experience, you will find *your* definition of success."

You can see that some people have viewed success through an intrinsic lens, while others required extrinsic factors to define success. The only wrong method of defining success for yourself is a failure to do so at all. Without knowing how you define success, you will be unable to develop a vision and set goals that move you in the direction that will provide lasting fulfillment with your work.

2.2 GOALS WILL GET YOU TO THE NEXT LEVEL

2.2.1 THE IMPORTANCE OF GOAL-SETTING

ONE OF THE most effective ways of growing your business is through goal-setting. Setting goals is a good way to clarify your focus, measure your progress, and track your achievements. Goals present a chance to push yourself to the outer limits of your comfort zone to take calculated risks. The more you are willing to stretch yourself, the greater gains you will make over the long term. Creating a plan for sustainable and intentional growth is the whole purpose of goal-setting and accompanying vision statements. By undertaking these tasks, you can aid your law practice in reaching new levels of success.[1]

The system I prefer for goal-setting incorporates S.M.A.R.T. goals:

- **Specific**: Goals should be simplistically written and define what you will do.
- **Measurable**: Goals should be measurable so that you have tangible evidence that you have accomplished the goal. Usually, the entire goal statement is a measure for the project, but there are

usually several short-term or smaller measurements built into the goal.

- **Achievable**: Goals should stretch you slightly so you feel challenged, but defined well enough so that you can achieve them. You must possess the appropriate knowledge, skills, and abilities needed to achieve the goal.
- **Results-focused**: Goals should measure outcomes, not activities.
- **Time-bound**: Goals should be linked to a timeframe that creates a practical sense of urgency, or results in tension between the current reality and the vision of the goal. Without that tension, the goal is unlikely to produce a relevant outcome.[2]

Since the Fall of 2016, I have been diligent in setting goals for the upcoming year. The experience has been transformative for me in both my law and writing practices. I have not met all the goals I've set. Far from it. Maybe I've met half of them. But I'm certain that the practice of goal-setting has propelled me further down the path of success than where I would have been otherwise. That's the importance of goal-setting, that it drives you toward achieving a particular objective and obtaining results you want to accomplish.

Be particularly mindful of the goals you think are too ambitious. They are sneaky. Even though they often go unfulfilled, they have the effect of driving you harder and creating momentum for future success. Whether you experience the particular joy of meeting a goal within the time parameters you set can be inconsequential. You should look instead at what having the goal enabled you to accomplish that you may not have done otherwise.

Consider these thoughts from Sonya Highfield of Real World Creatives about coming to terms with her ambitions:

> The best thing I did to up level my business was acknowledge I had big dreams and accept I was allowed to pursue those. Once I realized I am just as exceptional, and human, as everyone making Oprah/Beyonce/Marie Forleo money, then I could direct my businesses in a way that aligned with my desires. I felt at ease charging more, working more hours, and talking about my goals and accomplishments. It's okay to set crazy-high goals no matter where you are in life. The truth is there's room for all of us to be wildly successful.[3]

LOOKING TO THE PAST FOR EVIDENCE OF SUCCESS

When I first bought the moleskin notebook where I write down ideas, two of my earliest entries pertained to goals for my law practice for 2017 and goals for my law blog for the last five months of 2016 and into 2017. I had launched the blog in June 2016, and up until August, traffic had been ... meager, stilted, inconsistent. So my goals for the rest of 2016 were humble: have daily traffic on the website; have at least one guest writer on the blog; and publish 6-8 posts per month.

So what happened the rest of the year? In November, I had 94 visitors to the blog and published 19 articles. In December, 393 visitors came to the site, and I published 17 articles.

At the same time that I committed those 2016 goals to paper, I also developed my goals for 2017: average 100 visitors were month; publish 2 articles per week; and publish my transportation litigation primer e-book. Based on where my blog was positioned when I made the goals, they felt big at the time. As it turned out, because of several factors (including the relationships I had formed), my goals should have been more ambitious. By the end of 2017, the blog had more than 2,200 visitors per month, and I met my other goals as well.

You may look at those numbers and think that they're still pretty meager. And I won't disagree with you. At that point my law blog was a fragile seedling, something I was just trying to keep alive. It has since developed into a profitable business on its own, a source of business referrals for my law practice, and the foundation on which I have built my author business.

I have also implemented goals when it comes to my book sales. I set five goals for 2019. One of them was ambitious, and even at the time of setting it, I was unsure whether it was achievable. I set out to sell 1,000 copies of my books in 2019. Knowing that my goal would be difficult to accomplish, I put a plan in place to increase the likelihood of selling my books. I promoted it on social media, did podcast interviews, had others with audiences review and help promote the book. I did all the things that I had time to do while still running a hectic litigation practice. And by the end of 2019, I had sold about 500 books. Half what I had set out to do, but more than I would have done had I not had a goal to push toward.

LOOKING TO OTHERS FOR EVIDENCE OF GOAL-SETTING'S EFFECTIVENESS

Rather than tell you more stories about my own goal-setting successes and failures, I have reached out to two other lawyers. I asked them about what goal-setting has enabled them to accomplish with their businesses in the last year and what they have in mind for their futures.

- **Chris Ambrose of Harvest Legal, Emporia, KS**

I've known Chris for a couple of years now, and we have had innumerable conversations about the efforts he's been making to grow his law practice. He's taken specific steps to be more productive and delegate work to increase his efficiency. These measures have paid off by enabling him to become more profitable and have room for growth.

Ambrose explained, "This past year I had set up in my practice management software some billing and time goals, which I've been able to keep. If anything I've underestimated them." *Underestimated them* is an understatement. I can't remember a month in 2019 in which Chris hasn't met his billable goals well before the month is out. He's able to track that because he set Specific and Measurable goals. Here's what that is looking like for his year as a whole.

At the time of our interview in October, Ambrose projected, "I will hit yearly goal by mid-November. As it stands, I'm 18% over my year to date goal as of today." Ambrose has been able to do this while still spending tons of time with his growing family and doing competitive cycling (which he's called a part-time job). Because he knows exactly what he wants to accomplish, Chris can do that without it having to come at the expense of his personal life.

With 2019 having gone so well, I asked Ambrose what he has in mind for 2020. He responded, "For next year, we have implemented some new task tracking tools to help me better stay proactively on top of stuff so I don't accidentally fall behind due to the sheer amount of work I do. Also, I'll be continuing my practice management goals with more billable hours, and continuing to train my assistant to lean on her further for helping me get rid of all the non-billable work I can. Finally, the last goal will be to work on content creation in a meaningful way and not be so wrapped up in the work I have that I don't work on expanding my business still."

But his next sentences are the one that I found both most revealing and something I can identify with. "I'm thinking I'm going to up my billable goal by 11% next year. Part of me is anxious I won't hit it."

Good! If you're not setting goals that create some uncertainty, you're not being ambitious enough. Your goals should scare you a bit. The importance of goal-setting is that it stretches you beyond your comfort level. Entrepreneur Bedros Keuilian has this to say about ambitious goal-setting: "If you aren't scared, it means you're in your comfort zone. It's impossible to grow in your comfort zone, so now's the time to go charging out of it. Because big thinking leads to big results."[4]

- ## "Young Litigator" in the Wild West

If you aren't following Young Litigator (@young_litigator) on Twitter, you are missing out on someone who has taken her practice by storm in a short time. She is transparent about both her good and bad experiences. And she is exemplary in the ways she conducts herself and her law practice.

Knowing that YL had experienced an incredible 2019, I asked her to share what that had looked like.

When I started 2019, I looked at how my 2018 ended and what I could do to grow in the upcoming year. Still newly solo and not entirely sure how to measure those goals and growth, I looked mainly to my 2018 numbers (I started solo March 2018). I hired my full time paralegal in Sept. 2018 and this is when I really started setting monthly minimums to meet instead of just flying by the seat of my pants.

I surpassed my first few months goals and continued that into 2019. Just trying to be a little better every month, being more cognizant of billable hours, and overall have a better monthly average for the full year revenue than the previous year.

But that doesn't mean that the success she was experiencing came without any difficulties.

A hiccup I had in those goals was growing in office space. It was one of my priority goals for 2019 as I had outgrown the tiny space with a FT employee. Early on in the year I moved from a 1 office + reception suite to a 2 office + conference room + reception + supply closet/workroom suite. I had more than tripled in square footage, and it was in prime downtown district with other businesses.

The setback was that the expenses went up nearly 3x and added the expense of parking spaces, plus purchasing new furniture to fill the space, etc. So while I was steadily increasing my monthly revenues and I had met my goal of growing in space, I had the added expenses that were setting me back from making more take-home money.

After she ran into the problem, YL did exactly what she needed to overcome it -- she created a plan for her business and set goals.

To overcome this, I realized I couldn't just do a little better each month than my 2018 average. I needed to grow exponentially. First, I set guidelines for my paralegal in billing each week. She had really just been doing a lot of non-billable admin work before that.

I set guidelines for myself in billing each week. I also increased my retainers for family law matters and only took those that could pay those higher retainers. This cut back on any outstanding unpaid bills. I also focused on advertising--

where I should cut (I cut my monthly SEO package) and where I should spend (I added google ads for the first time, increased my Avvo boosts, and did a tv package). I focused on getting more contingency cases-PI and SSDI.

In 3 short months, I had so much new contingency business, I was turning a lot away. The little bit of advertising money was well spent.

In the end, what has resulted from all this growth for YL?

Now, my 2019 monthly average revenue is up 65% from last year, while my expenses are up 33%. So I'm still managing growth just in different terms. And in a new office I love that I can continue to grow in.

LOOKING FORWARD FOR FUTURE SUCCESS

Dr. Gail Matthews of Dominican University in California studied goal-setting that revealed people are 42% more likely to achieve goals for the mere act of having written them down.[5]

It really is as simple as that. The singular act of writing down your goals increases your odds of success by more than 40%. Even if you're skeptical about the importance of goal-setting, isn't it worth doing? If you haven't set written goals before, what have you got to lose?

If you have been setting goals, how are they coming along? Have you put your list where it's staring at you every day beckoning you to take affirmative steps that will enable you to achieve those goals? Or has it been a rough start? Persevere. Keep plodding forward. The importance of goal-setting is that your goals serve as fixed points that help you navigate your practice and instruct the decisions you make.

Start planning now to give yourself the greatest likelihood

of success. And don't be timid about being ambitious. Richard Branson is quoted as saying, "When people are placed in positions slightly above what they expect, they are apt to excel." Do this for yourself. Push yourself to excellence by increasing your expectations for yourself one goal at a time.

2.2.2 MONITOR GOALS WITH KEY PERFORMANCE INDICATORS

FOR 2019, I set as one of my goals generating a certain amount of revenue through my billable hours. To make that more manageable, I broke it down into how much I needed to bill each day to attain my yearly goal. This type of metric is a Key Performance Indicator (KPI) that would enable me to demonstrate how effectively I was achieving my business objective: being profitable.

I established that I wanted to generate a specific amount of revenue per day for 236 days. That wasn't just a random number of days. Here's how I arrived at it — there were 251 workdays in 2019 (excluding weekends and holidays), so I figured between vacations, speaking events, attending conferences, and sick days, I should factor in missing up to 15 workdays for sickness or vacations.

My next step was to modify a spreadsheet that would enable me to keep up with those figures. Because I already had a spreadsheet for my time entries, all I had to do was add a column to my spreadsheet and plug in a formula that would allow me every day as I entered my time to see how much money my time entries amounted to each day. The only value I had been looking at previously is the number of hours I was working each day. But since my rate varies by client, that one indicator was insufficient to inform me about how much revenue I was generating each day. I needed a new metric to monitor my progress toward my goal.

By using this metric to track my performance, I could surpass my goal. Not only that, I knew by August that as long as I kept tracking consistently with what I'd done the first eight months of the year that by the time the final bills went out for the year in December, I would have exceeded my goal. Here's what that looked like specifically, broken down by month, number of workdays in that month, and percentage of billable revenue generated compared to my goal.

- January (21) - 114%
- February (19) - 106%
- March (21) - 97%
- April (22) - 97%
- May (22) - 105%
- June (20) - 108%
- July (22) - 94%
- August (22) - 105%
- September (20) - 87%
- October (22) - 124%
- November (19) - 109%
- December (20) - 100%

USING METRICS TO MEASURE S.M.A.R.T. GOALS AND KPIS

We use this data to show how it can help monitor S.M.A.R.T.

goals with appropriate metrics (KPIs). My **Specific** goal was to generate $X amount of billable revenue in 2019. Since that is a number, it is **Measurable**. When I set the goal in 2018, I was pretty sure it was **Achievable** since I was being made a partner and would get a rate increase along with my new position, but it was an 18% increase over my goal from the year before. The goal was **Results-focused** in that it reflected the amount of work performed each day, rather than the individual tasks that comprised the number. Finally, the goal was **Time-bound** in that I had only a finite period to achieve it.

When goals and KPIs are clearly defined, they enable you to make sure that your daily activities align with your greater objectives for your practice. This alignment is the critical link between your daily performance and overall business success.[1] Without goals or key performance indicators to provide you direction, you may be working hard, but paddling in circles and making no progress toward success. Settings goals and monitoring with KPIs ensures that your actions resonate with your intentions and move you toward a successful outcome.

Not all KPIs are this immediately quantifiable though. For each of the last three years, I have had as one of my goals to add one new insurance or corporate client to my book of business. While that meets all the S.M.A.R.T. criteria, achieving the goal is less straight forwarding than making sure I generate a certain amount of revenue each day so that I make my number by year's end. The actions required to bring in a new corporate client are more nebulous and will be part of the discussion in Part 3 of this book.

By having the goal of adding a client I can keep in mind that there are things I need to do on a regular basis to achieve it. I have to continue to market myself and my firm, maintain existing relationships with clients, keep up my presence in my business and social communities, and push into new spaces. These all require specific actions that, while not quantifiable, are identifiable. And if necessary, I could create an actionable plan to track whether I'm progressing toward the goal.

ALIGNING GOALS WITH BUSINESS OBJECTIVES

Whatever your specific goals, they should align with your vision for your business. To that end, you can ask yourself these questions to help yourself better understand the context of creating KPIs that will be effective for you.[2]

- **What is my vision for my practice?**

Hopefully, you've already put some thought into this one and maybe even written some things down. If not, now is a good time to do so.

Each of the goals that I discussed above is essential to the growth and success of my law practice -- continuing to develop client relationships and being profitable. It is imperative that your goals and KPIs align with your greater vision for your business.

If your KPIs are not integral to the practice's success, you will be "aiming for a target that fails to address a business outcome. That means that, at best, you're working towards a goal that has no impact for your organization. At worst, it will result in your business wasting time, money and other resources that would have best been directed elsewhere."[3]

- **What metrics will signify that I am progressing toward my vision?**

I've identified above how I used metrics to monitor my

progress. But your goals are likely different than mine. Maybe you want to increase your profitability by 10% or increase the number of phone calls you're receiving from potential clients by 25%. Determine how you can put metrics in place that will allow you to analyze your performance in that area.

- **What strategies should I implement to achieve my goals?**

Once you've established the goals and KPIs that will move you toward your vision, you have to identify strategies you can deploy to achieve them. This will take time, creativity, and diligence. Once you put your processes in place, you will have to monitor for their effectiveness.

For example, when I released my second book, *Stop Putting Out Fires*, I set a goal to sell 1,000 copies of it in 2019. One of my strategies for selling more books was to run some ad campaigns on Facebook and Amazon.

I knew there would be a learning curve. Amazon was still in the early stages of letting smaller players access Amazon Marketing Services, so I would have to make changes to my ads in response to the changes it made to its system. It has been a process that requires regular monitoring and adjustment.

With Facebook, I knew that many authors have had great success running ads on the platform. There are whole courses and author websites built around how to sell books through Facebook ads. So I devised a couple of ad campaigns and spent some money trying to sell books that way. I am pretty certain I didn't sell a single book as a result. Maybe I wasn't reaching my audience, maybe I didn't create an enticing ad or have the right copy. It's hard to say *why* I wasn't getting any results. But the evidence was clear that nothing was happening as a result of the Facebooks ads, so I stopped running them.

If I hadn't been monitoring my strategy for results, I may have continued to dump resources into a method that wasn't showing any returns. Instead, I chalked it up to a learning experience, pivoted into the next thing, and focused on things that were working.

- **Can you access the data to monitor your KPIs?**

Goals and KPIs are only as effective as your ability to track them. You will need to make sure you have the software or data available to you to keep up with the information. "When you're deciding which KPIs to set up, plan how you'll capture the information you need. Net profit requires a different set of data than customer satisfaction, for example, and requires access to different systems."[4]

The metrics you need may be as simple as revenue and profitability. You may want to look at more advanced data like comparing profitability across various practice areas or lines of business. You'll have to make sure you have access to that information. If you want to monitor customer satisfaction, you may have to create a survey or other tool that makes it measurable, and then entice customers to participate and give honest feedback.

WHAT GETS MEASURED GETS DONE ... SOMETIMES

The axiom that "what gets measured gets done" is only partly true. Your goals and KPIs will not achieve themselves. While it's true that the mere act of writing down a goal boosts the likelihood of it being achieved, a regular awareness of your KPIs will prompt actions that result in achievement.

Every November, I write down my goals for the upcoming

year. In fact, yesterday (as I type this), I spent about 45 minutes committing to paper my goals for my law practice and writing business for 2020. These goals had been percolating for a few weeks. Now it's time to consider what KPIs I can implement to track those goals.

2.2.3 MAKE YOUR OWN OPPORTUNITIES

FIVE MILE CREEK is stalked by a yellow crowned night heron. Every morning she fishes there for crawfish, wading its waters looking for a good spot. One morning, I took my camera so I could watch her more closely. This is what I saw.

The heron perched on a submerged rock and waited, watching. For long minutes, she stood motionless. Water bugs and leaves floated past her. A school of minnows swam by. Still she stood there, statuesque.

Abruptly, she plunged her head through the surface of the creek. Just as quickly she pulled herself upright with a crawfish wriggling in her beak. She tilted her head back, and the prey disappeared. Then she returned to her stillness.

The heron used her experience to scout a fishing spot where she was most likely to succeed. She found a narrow channel where the water funneled between two rocks. The current ran a bit stronger there, but the critters beneath the surface had little room to move laterally and avoid capture.

She was patient. She didn't take the first thing that came along. She didn't settle for less than she had set out for. She waited. When her target made its appearance, she was poised to strike.

The heron made her own opportunity. She did not sit in her nest and ruminate about her hunger. She did not wait for her partner (assuming for the sake of illustration that yellow crowned night herons have partners) to bring her the breakfast he caught. No, she got out there early in the morning and positioned herself so when the crawfish awoke and started their morning, she was already in place. She didn't disturb or alarm them by getting into position. She made her opportunity and increased her likelihood of success.

You and I have to do the same thing. No one is as invested in your success as you are. So it follows that you should not rely on others to create opportunities for you or passively hope that opportunities present themselves. You have to seek them out and put yourself in position to capitalize on them.

In May 2017, I was getting ready to head to a conference that was a few weeks away. As I always do, I was going through the list of attendees to see if there was anyone I knew or might want to meet up with. I reached out to the head of claims for an insurance carrier to see if we could have dinner while at the conference. He responded that he'd be glad to. They had just started writing insurance in Alabama and were looking for a lawyer to partner with. We made dinner plans.

A week before the conference, the head of claims called me. One of their insureds had experienced a catastrophic loss, and he wanted to know if I could help them. So I started handling their work before we'd even met in person. And we've been working together for the last three years.

If I hadn't made that initial call and created an opportunity, I wouldn't have been able to help them when they needed it weeks later. They would have found someone to do their work. But you can be sure, it would not have been me.

Do you have a new practice area or line of business you want to expand into? A new client you want to work with? A new business strategy you want to implement?

Make your own opportunity. No one is more interested than you in seeing that you succeed. Do your market research. Discern how you might be able to build up trust equity with your potential client and begin to form a relationship. Do the work to position yourself for success. Do what is necessary to make your own opportunity and then capitalize on it.

2.3 IMPLEMENT EFFICIENT WORK HABITS

2.3.1 DO WHAT YOU MUST AND DELEGATE THE REST

DELEGATION IS AN IMPORTANT MANAGEMENT SKILL. You have to prioritize between the work you *could* be doing versus the work you *should* be doing. In my law practice, I have a sharp distinction: if I can't bill a client for a particular task, someone else needs to be doing it. Now there are obvious caveats to this — e.g., marketing and relationship-building work that only you can do — but the principle still stands.

You are in a service business and there are tasks to be performed that your clients won't pay you to do, so someone else should be doing them. Otherwise, you are taking income out of your pocket and your practice's accounts by electing to do work that doesn't cause income.

There are those who say you should even delegate personal errands because your time is too valuable to be spent in that way. Donald Miller tells a story on his podcast, *Building a StoryBrand*, that a consultant once told him he should not even be mowing his own yard because the time that took is time he could have been working for clients and earning money for his business. That seems like a bridge too far to me. Yard work is a stress relief outlet for me. Every Saturday morning for nine months out of the year, I get 90-120 minutes of solitude, where I can listen to podcasts or audiobooks or just let my mind float for a while. That particular personal, non-billable task is worth more to me than the money I could be earning while doing it.

WHAT WORK TO DELEGATE

There is a balance to be struck. But let's look at specific ways that delegating administrative or non-income related tasks can lead to a more profitable business. During his presidency, Dwight D. Eisenhower faced a barrage of decisions to be made every day. He developed a system that has become known as the Eisenhower Matrix to help contend with the overload. It advised how he should respond to a situation that arose.

He created a box with four quadrants. Where a task fell within the matrix determined how it would be handled, or whether it would be handled at all.

	Urgent	Not Urgent
Important	Quadrant 1 Urgent and important Handle it immediately.	Quadrant 2 Important but not urgent Schedule a time to handle it.
Unimportant	Quadrant 3 Urgent but unimportant Delegate it to someone else.	Quadrant 4 Unimportant and not urgent Eliminate it.

Eisenhower Matrix

If something is both urgent and important, you should handle it immediately. Last spring, I got a call from a client that one of their trucks had been involved in a wreck that was likely to result in a fatality. They needed me to go out to the site to coordinate all the things that needed to happen with their driver and vehicle to be compliant with the Federal Motor Carrier Safety Regulations. This was a time-sensitive matter that was critical for the client. I dropped what I was doing and headed out.

If a matter is important but not pressing, you schedule a time to do it. When you get a scheduling order from a court and see that your dispositive motion deadline is 90 days away, you schedule time to work on your motion for summary judgment within the next 89 days. It isn't necessary for you to stop everything and start drafting that motion and gathering exhibits immediately. The task is important, but there's plenty of time to get it done.

An issue that is urgent but unimportant enables you to delegate it to others, whether that is to support staff, a paralegal, or an associate. Entering billable time into the system needs to be done regularly, but you aren't the person who needs to do it. There are plenty of non-billable tasks that need to be done promptly but don't necessarily need *your* attention. These are things you should delegate to others.

Finally, if something neither important nor urgent, don't bother doing it at all. Don't even delegate it. Just eliminate the task. I used to keep paper files for all my cases. They included correspondence, pleadings, discovery documents, medical records, and so on. Every document that became a part of the case went into the paper file. It took an extraordinary amount of space. But technology and the cheap prices of digital storage have made paper files like that unnecessary for my practice. The only time I use paper documents is in preparing for depositions, preparing to argue motions, or getting ready for trial.

And for those things, I can print the documents as needed. So I have eliminated the unimportant and non-urgent task of printing and filing paper documents for my cases. This has freed staff up to work on other tasks delegated to them.

DELEGATING HELPS YOU MANAGE YOUR TIME MORE EFFECTIVELY

As a lawyer, you are the engine for the success of your practice. The undercurrent that should affect your decision-making is "How much income can I generate today?" That may be through billable work, developing cases to try or settle, or networking with clients and potential clients. However your practice is structured, you are tasked with its financial viability. You can only shepherd that if you are focusing on the income-driving work.

Sending out invoices, maintaining records of cash flow, and handling payroll are a drain on your time and mental resources. You can take back those resources by hiring someone to handle your firm's finances.[1] Even if you aren't in a position to hire someone full time, there are options for virtual assistants and bookkeepers, whose time you "rent" for an allotted amount each month.

Find as many ways as possible to clear out your mental space and free up time to do the important work of building your law practice. Only you can drive your cases forward, maintain relationships with existing clients, and develop new relationships. The necessary tasks that don't fall within those broad categories may be delegable. And by delegating this work, you are positioning yourself to be more effective by increasing your capacity for creative energy and profitability.

DELEGATING ENABLES YOU TO MAINTAIN YOUR CREATIVE ENERGY

Bring in people to do the things you're not passionate about. For every construction defect case, there are dozens of depositions. Contractors, sub-contractors, experts, the plaintiffs. Do you have any idea how mind-numbing it can be to summarize twenty depositions about defective windows? I do because I've done it. My clients require reporting about depositions in cases. So deposition summaries are essential tasks in these cases. But they often take hours and can be a drain on your creative energy. Delegate the task.

Doing so enables you to pour your creative energy into the higher priority tasks of case strategy. If you took the deposition, *you* don't need to summarize it to know whether it was beneficial to your case or problematic. But you likely are the person who needs to develop either the measures to counterbalance the harmful testimony or use the benefits of it.

By shedding the necessary but mundane work, you free yourself up to do work that requires a greater deal of skill and experience. Work that only you can do.

DELEGATING INCREASES YOUR PROFITABILITY

Profitability is the key to the survival and growth of any business. You can only do so much work in a day before you reach a saturation point. Eventually, you get to the point that you can no longer take on any more work. It is only by delegating work to others that you can increase your capacity for more work, and therefore your profitability. Consider what Becky Mollenkamp has to say about reaching this saturation point and her response:

I reached a point where I could no longer take on new clients and more work without putting in a ridiculous number of hours each week. Instead of saying no, I decided to find a younger professional in my field to whom I could subcontract the work. I pay her a reasonable fee that's still below what I earn on the project. It requires some oversight on my part, but the arrangement allows me to continue adding new clients and gives me time to focus on growing the business even more.[2]

Delegating can be difficult. We inherently trust ourselves to handle things appropriately more than we trust others. To force ourselves into delegating, we have to consider the vision that we established for our practices and the specific goals we would like to achieve. We must recognize that the way forward is through growth, which comes with its own pains. Sometimes that involves training others to do the work we have previously done ourselves and trusting them to handle it competently.

Alyssa Gregory underwent such a transition in her business: "Whether you have employees, subcontractors or family pitching in, learning how to delegate effectively can be the difference between reaching new heights and burning out. Many small business owners are accustomed to doing a variety of things themselves instead of enlisting the help of others, so it can be challenging to identify the tasks you don't need to do yourself and assign the work to someone else. Once you overcome the challenge, though, you will have more time to dedicate to what you do best — grow your business."[3]

There is work you can and must do yourself. Some of it requires immediate attention. More of it can be scheduled for the future. More still can be delegated to associates, support staff, or even virtual assistants. And there is some work that can be eliminated. Deciphering among these things and handling them appropriately increases your capacity to do the work that only you can do. It increases your profitability by allowing you to take on more work through delegation of non-essential tasks to others.

2.3.2 BATCH YOUR PROCESSES TO WORK MORE EFFICIENTLY

ONCE A MONTH, I send out an email to the folks who subscribe to my email list. A few months ago, I noticed a particular auto-responder that I got from one lawyer who subscribes to the list:

> I only check my email twice each day. My goal is to reply to yours within one business day of receipt. If you need a quicker reply, please contact my office manager at [email address].
>
> If you are a client please log into MyCase using your login credentials and send me a message there, and please remember to copy the paralegal assigned to your matter when you do! Client messages within MyCase receive higher priorities than email.

This intrigued me. But it wasn't until I was reading Tim Ferriss's *The 4-Hour Workweek* in which he discusses email batching that I decided to look into the idea further. One aspect of doing so was reaching out to the lawyer, Merrianne Dean, whose email auto-responder had first piqued my interest.

EMAIL BATCHING WITH MERRIANNE DEAN

JWR: Where did you learn about batching tasks, and specifically emails? How long have you been batching tasks?

MD: I don't recall exactly when this idea first caught my eye. It's a recurring theme in many of the articles I've read related to increasing efficiency.

JWR: Other than emails, what other tasks do you batch?

MD: I try to batch my phone calls and meetings in the late afternoon as much as possible. My ability to engage in creative writing plummets around that time. My ability to talk with others on the phone or in meetings is the best use of my time later in the day.

JWR: What caused you to want to give batching emails a try?

MD: It became obvious to me that responding to emails, texts, and phone calls at the time they initially appear is a serious disruption to my thought processes and my ability to stay focused on completing the other work a lawyer needs to do to serve her clients. I'd seen the articles I mentioned above and decided something had to change.

JWR: Has email batching had the intended effect on your work?

MD: Absolutely.

JWR: Have you had any response to your email message about checking emails twice daily from clients or opposing counsel?

MD: So far, it's all been positive — usually the response is that the other person is going to try the same technique in their own practice.

We use a cloud based practice management service called MyCase and all of our client communications occur within that environment which ensures that the conversations all stay in one location for easy reference — instead of digging through a full email box or taking the time to set up a series of "rules" to move client emails to sub folders. I encourage anyone who hasn't tried one of these services to check them out — there are at least 4 main contenders that each have slightly different features so it shouldn't be difficult to find one you and, more importantly, your clients like.

JWR: How has batching effected your productivity and efficiency?

MD: As you might imagine, from my comments above, it's improved both areas of focus.

JWR: Have you experienced any negative consequences from batching emails?

MD: Not so far. It's kind of a no-brainer once you give it a try.

JWR: What recommendations or advice would you have for others who either want to learn more about batching tasks or who want to implement such a system?

MD: Come on in, the water's fine. Pick a logical time for accomplishing batched tasks and block that time in your calendar — as a reminder to you, when you're getting used to the change, and to ensure your staff don't try to schedule appointments or meetings during those time blocks. Also, remember to stay flexible — sometimes you're going to need to deviate.

JWR: What would you say to people like me who are interested in batching emails and only checking our inboxes once or twice per day, but are scared or reluctant to pull the trigger?

MD: See my comments above. Just do it. If it doesn't work for you, there's obviously no reason you can't do something different. Not being immediately available to the hoards of people who would like you to be at their beck and call is freeing. Ideally, we work at whatever job we do because we enjoy the work. If responding to emails, texts, and phone calls isn't part of what gives you joy, or interferes with your ability to do the work that gives you joy, it's up to you to control it.

Another aspect of controlling your work environment is to make sure clients and opposing counsel know that you are NOT available evenings and weekends. I've declined work when the client insists on being able to communicate 24/7. Really, there is nothing I can do outside of regular business hours that will benefit my clients or their cases that isn't better done during regular business hours. The single exception to this is during trial, when it's often necessary to work into the evening or on weekends to prepare for the next trial day.

IS BATCHING TASKS RIGHT FOR YOU?

We should all monitor whether we could be more productive. Keep an eye out for whether you can improve your utilization rates. Maybe it would be worthwhile for you to consider batching your emails and other tasks to squeeze more work out of your day without increasing the time you spend working.

Batching tasks eliminates the distraction caused by incessant inbox chime. It allows you to respond to arising issues on your own schedule, rather than someone else's. Task batching enables you to stay focused on the deep work you are (or should be) pursuing. Perhaps this is the most important thing — it minimizes distractions.

The days that I find distressing are when I've been in the office for nine hours and look down to discover that my timesheet only reflects 5.6 hours of billable work. Where did the other 3.4 hours go? They're lost to the great abyss of inefficiency and distraction. Lost to me handling non-billable work that I should have handed off to support staff. Or maybe I've just been piddling around trying to avoid doing certain work. Whatever the answer, the result is frustrating.

Cal Newport wrote in *Deep Work*: "The ability to perform deep work is becoming increasingly rare at exactly the same time it is becoming increasingly valuable in our economy. As a consequence, the few who cultivate this skill, and then make it the core of their working life, will thrive." Be among the few who have the capacity and willingness to engage in deep work. By doing so, you will put yourself in an advantageous position to be more effective at your craft.

Distraction is persistent and pervasive. We like to think of ourselves as effective multi-taskers, but we are operating under a constant state of inefficiency. A study performed at York University yielded results revealing that when we are multi-tasking, we decrease our efficacy by 11%.[1] But more than that, we also distract those who are around us. Our inefficiencies deteriorate the work quality and efficiency of all those within our immediate environment. So if there are tactics we can deploy to make ourselves (and as a byproduct, those around us) more effective and less distracted, it would seem foolish not to at least consider implementing them into our workflow.

PART 3

YOUR CLIENTS ARE
YOUR BUSINESS

THAT STAR POWER

About two-thirds of the way through World 1-1 of Super Mario Bros., you jump up and punch one of the question mark boxes. Rather than a coin or fire flower, a star elevates out of the top of it and starts flitting across the screen. If you can catch it, you increase your speed, jumping ability, and become invulnerable to attack. The lightest touch of your opponents sends them flying off the screen, kaput.

Clients are your star power. And just as elusive. When you land one, you get star power. And like the stars in Super Mario Bros., you have to know where to find clients, put yourself in position to obtain them, and know what to do with them once you've got them.

The best way to get the attention of potential clients is to set yourself apart from the competition. Think about the average lawyer. They're probably not particularly good at their job. They are unimpressive. Indistinguishable from the mass of other lawyers. And half of lawyers are worse than that. Does that sound about right?

By you reading this book and taking affirmative steps to

improve your craft, I'd venture to guess that you don't see yourself in that crowd. You envision yourself as set apart, above average. That you care enough to improve suggests that you are not (or at the very least, do not want to be considered) among the herd. But how can you distinguish yourself from the average lawyer? From the average law firm?

"BE DIFFERENT, NOT BETTER"

When I was about a third of the way through the writing of this book, I was driving to work on the first cold morning of the year in Birmingham. The latest episode of Jeff Goins's *The Portfolio Life* podcast was playing. The subtitle, "Be Different, Not Better," piqued my interest in this particular episode. A few minutes into the episode, Jeff made the statement, "The ones who stand out are the ones who are brave enough to pave their own way."[1]

I thought, *Holy cow! That's exactly what I'm talking about.* Trying to improve on what someone else has built gets you only so far. You can only put so much of yourself into someone else's construction.

The better path, the more innovative path is to be different. To be uncommon. Not to do the same thing better than someone else has already done it, but to do a different thing. Potential clients may have difficulty distinguishing from the outside whether one lawyer is *better* than another, but they can certainly recognize when one lawyer is doing things differently than others. Approach your law practice in a unique way that suits your skill set and meets the needs of your clients in a way that they haven't experienced before.

You will have failures. That is unavoidable, and we've discussed it already. There is an adage that pertains to innovation and failure: "The plains are littered with the bodies of pioneers." Fortunately for us, we are pioneers of ideas and experiments. We get the chance to learn from our failures, from what did not work. We can either adapt the failures or throw them out altogether. We aren't facing literal snake bites and dysentery like the settlers we unintentionally killed off playing Oregon Trail in elementary school. (Am I dating myself too much with that reference?)

But even your failures are only failures if you allow them to be by choosing to learn nothing from them. They represent opportunity for growth and innovation. They build resonance. Your failures help mold your successes. And your successes will have more substance because they derive from the traits that make you uncommon. They reflect you, rather than those you thought it necessary to emulate.

In this last part of the book, consider what you can do to distinguish yourself from the competition. What you can do differently to give your clients an experience that keeps them coming back. That keeps them choosing to work with you.

Finally, I want to leave you with this from Gary Keller's *The One Thing*: "Anyone who dreams of an uncommon life eventually discovers there is no choice but to seek an uncommon approach to living it." Substitute *law practice* for *life*. Go after an uncommon law practice — one that is healthy, robust, focused, and client-centric. This is an uncommon approach but one that will empower you to reach your unfettered potential.

3.1 THE IMPORTANCE OF ATTRACTING POTENTIAL CLIENTS

3.1.1 HELP POTENTIAL CLIENTS FIND YOU

IT DOESN'T MATTER how good of a lawyer you are if your potential clients can't find you. There are effectively no phone books anymore. When people need a lawyer, they go to a search engine and punch in "bankruptcy lawyer Wilmington NC". If you're a bankruptcy lawyer in Wilmington, North Carolina, you'd better have enough of an internet presence that you're on the first page of search results.

Research has shown that 91.5% of people never take their search queries beyond the first page of search results.[1] Think about your own experiences, how often do you scroll all the way down to the bottom of a search page and click on the 2 or any of the other successive numbers?

Having a website is essential, but that alone is not enough to ensure that people who need your services are finding you. You should be doing content marketing on your website to increase your presence and improve your opportunities to be found. By "content marketing," I mean that you should be consistently creating and distributing content to your clients and potential clients that is valuable and relevant to their needs. This will allow you to attract and acquire a specific audience to drive interest, engagement, and (most importantly) profitability.

My law blog is an example of content marketing. I'm providing practical information about different ways for lawyers to manage their clients, cases, and law practice. I'm not actively trying to sell my readers something every day, but I do hope to provide enough value that they will see more value in buying my books.

As concerns your law practice, you should do your content marketing to help attract potential clients and providing them with information that will identify their problems and show them you have the expertise to resolve their issues.

Content marketing is important for several reasons. Search engines prefer when websites are often updated (meaning more organic search traffic to your site). Content marketing provides information that shows your expertise. It helps you foster a relationship and build trust with your potential clients. But most importantly, it provides ways for people to find your website.[2]

You don't have to write a blog though. Video and audio are perfectly good ways to distribute content and ideas. Search engines are now indexing audio content just like they've been doing for years with written content. Podcasting can now provide you the same SEO benefits that writing has historically done. Regardless of your chosen media, the information you're sharing should be both beneficial and interesting in a way that will drive people to want to work with you.

Content marketing is a way to provide value and building up trust equity with potential clients. It also provides you a platform to exhibit your expertise on topics relevant to your practice areas.

If you're not engaging in content marketing to enable clients to find you and allow you to answer their questions, here's a primer about what content marketing is, what's it's not, and how to do it well. But before we jump into that, I want to provide evidence of the importance and effects of content marketing through the testimony of a business owner who has seen a change in their own sector.

Alexis Shaak of alexisnickcreates.com: "The best thing I did to level up my business was to educate my audience. For the longest time I was only focusing on promoting my work and my products to my current audience. As soon as I started sharing my knowledge and educating my audience, not only did my following and client base sky-rocket, it brought back repeat customers. Becoming an active voice in my field has been the best thing I have done for my business."[3]

WHAT DOES CONTENT MARKETING LOOK LIKE?

To help discuss content market in a law firm context, I spoke with Karin Conroy of Conroy Creative Counsel, who helps lawyers with their websites.

> **JWR:** In what ways is content marketing a long-game approach to success?

> **KC:** Content marketing is any strategic content your law firm shares with the public, such as social media posts, videos, or blogs. For most law firms, regularly scheduled blog posts can be helpful in engaging potential clients. However, blog posting should not be a haphazard free-for-all. Instead of writing whatever comes to mind on the day you scheduled a blog post to go out, a much more effective (and less stressful!) way to approach content marketing is by looking at the long game. You'll want to come up with a list of topics relevant to your practice, decide how often you want to post

and create a content marketing calendar that you can stick to. Commit to posting frequently to your blog for optimal results. We've all seen that website with the latest blog post from 2016 and it gives the visitor a bad impression of your ability to stay current and fresh.

JWR: Why should lawyers engage in content marketing?

KC: Content marketing lets law firms share how they are different and establish their authority on a subject. What makes you uniquely qualified to serve your clients? Content marketing should express your unique value proposition, whether that's your experience, your enthusiasm for the subject, your geographical location, or something else. A well thought out blog will explain your niche and attract your targeted audience. For example, if your firm specializes in estate planning, your blog should focus on questions pertaining to the problems that niche has, and how your firm can best solve those problems. A blog on a personal injury attorney's website will have different content. Here's your chance to attract your ideal clients and let them know that you're the right attorney to help solve their problem.

JWR: What does good content marketing look like?

KC: Good content marketing lets your visitor know they're in the right place. As they're reading your content, they should be saying to themselves, "This guys really understands me." Your message shouldn't come across as marketing. No one wants to be pitched to all the time. Instead of a salesman, picture yourself as a helpful colleague that has addressed their issue many times and knows answers to questions they haven't even thought of yet.

Tell a story instead of selling yourself. How do you do this? Put the human element into your content by sharing what attracted you to this type of law or why you are passionate about your specialization. By exposing your human side, you will draw in the reader and make a connection between yourself and your potential client. Think about your favorite advertisements and the story they tell. How did the story engage you? Content marketing is a powerful tool for converting website users to leads to clients.

You can also use your blog as a chance to boost SEO for your website by sprinkling in relevant keywords in your blog posts. Try using Google's Keyword Planner. For example, if you are a bankruptcy attorney in Los Angeles than using "bankruptcy attorney Los Angeles" or "bankruptcy lawyer LA" in your blogs can help boost your search rankings for those terms. However, don't overuse these keywords (commonly called "keyword stuffing"), as Google will downrank you for that.

Make it easily readable by ensuring the content is broken up into easily digestible chunks with bulleted lists and appropriate headers and sub-headers so your readers can scan through the post. The most important factors in content marketing are conveying your unique value proposition through storytelling, readability, and regularity.

JWR: What makes for bad content marketing?

KC: Bad content marketing is a nuisance. We all have businesses on our email lists and social media that constantly throw out their sales pitch without ever providing value. What happens to those companies? Most of us eventually unsubscribe from their emails or hide their posts from our feeds. You don't want to be the annoying pest!

No one enjoys constantly being pitched to, without any personalization or sense of what the business can offer you. Law firms need to carefully plan their content strategy to provide value for their target audience. Instead, offer your website visitors valuable content. For law firms, I highly recommend a white paper or legal guide on common questions. Make it clear your firm is the expert source for specific legal inquiries surrounding your specialization.

Lastly, just because you're writing a white paper does not mean your content has to be overly long, rambling, or full of jargon. This is an easy way to lose your readers. Make it easy to read for the average person who has little to no exposure to legal terms. That's it! Follow these rules to avoid bad content.

Good content marketing is not clickbait. It is not self-promotion. It is not a sales pitch. Good content marketing answers the questions your clients and potential clients have. It is a proven and effective strategy for helping clients find you and enabling you to grow your business.

THE REAL LIFE VALUE OF CONTENT MARKETING

In early 2017, I wrote about the effect of MCS-90 Endorsements on punitive damages exclusions. Now, that may sound like total gibberish to you. But to someone involved in insuring trucking companies or handling trucking litigation, it could become an important topic.

Almost two years later, I received an email from general counsel at an insurance company, saying that she had seen my blog post and had some questions. I called her and we talked about it.

Maybe that turns into a business relationship down the line, and maybe it doesn't. It may just be that I provided some information to someone in my industry and was able to help them out with a problem.

That's the power of content marketing. My writing answered a question that someone had. It prompted a conversation with a stranger. A relationship exists now where none existed before. Potential exists now for business development where there was none previously. No self-promotion. No catchy title without substance in the content. Just useful information that addressed a relevant issue for a colleague ... and potential client.

3.1.2 BUILD TRUST EQUITY BY WORKING FOR FREE

WHEN I LAUNCHED *Stop Putting Out Fires* in May 2019, I ran a giveaway in which I gave out free copies of my first book, *Building a Better Law Practice*. Doing this cost me time, money, and may have cost me sales from people who had purchased *Stop Putting Out Fires* and might have later bought *Building a Better Law Practice*. Instead, I gave the book to them for free.

So what is the upside of giving work away for free? Maybe I've instilled more loyalty among my readers. Perhaps I have built up some trust equity between us. The readers who received a free copy of my book obtained a greater value. But what I received from giving work away is intangible and possibly unknowable.

SHOULD YOU GIVE YOUR LEGAL SERVICES AWAY FOR FREE?

Since I'm in insurance defense, every day I'm working with claims adjusters all over the country who are handling large numbers of claims. Some work with claims in Alabama all the time, and others are either new to Alabama or only occasionally handle claims here. They may not be familiar with some of our quirkier laws or the real risk that some of our venues pose. This leaves them with a knowledge gap that hinders their ability to do their job with total efficacy.

I tell my clients (and potential clients) I work with that if they ever have a question about a claim they're handling in Alabama, they should always feel free to pick up the phone and give me a call. Don't worry about whether the matter is going into litigation now or will never get to litigation or get assigned to me. Just call me with your questions.

And they do. I field calls regularly with questions about Alabama law or evaluations of claims, in which I am giving work away for free. No doubt this has led me to give away dozens of hours of free advice to clients. But there is a benefit.

WHY AM I COMFORTABLE GIVING WORK AWAY FOR FREE?

Doing free work for clients may, in the short term, seem not to be a sound business decision. But if you look beyond the immediate billable hour and have a greater vision for your business and client relationships, you can see the value in giving your services away. To buy into giving work away, you have to adopt the abundance mindset we discussed in Part One – the belief that there's always more where that came from. Not every lawyer is willing to do this.

But if your clients know they can call you for a quick answer without you opening a new matter and billing them for it, you are likely going to be the first person they think of when they get ready to hire a lawyer again. And being top of mind for clients is of the utmost importance.

Branding and design consultant Sryna Myers has the same mindset: "The best thing I did to level up my business was to lead with generosity! I give free talks, free Q&A sessions in Facebook groups and do free calls where I give away a lot of advice. This has people giving me referrals, writing beautiful testimonials, and signing up for my services because they're left wondering, 'If the free stuff is this good... what will I get when I pay her?'"

Recently, my car started having some transmission problems. I took it to my local mechanic to have a look at. He and his guys spent about 45 minutes checking out the vehicle. Then he came back and told me that I needed to take it to the dealership because there seemed to be a problem beyond what they could handle for me. When I asked him how much I owed him, he said, "Nothing." I insisted that I needed to pay them for their time, but he still refused. I said, "Alright, thanks. I'll be back." He responded, "That's why I do it."

He had exactly the right frame of mind. He was willing to give away some of his work for free to build up loyalty and trust with a client. This was a means that served his long-term business goals and strengthened the relationship. He set himself apart from his competitors who may not have had that mindset and would have capitalized on the smaller transaction (and rightfully so).

Are you willing to sometimes perform a free service for your clients, knowing that it may over time lead you to give away thousands of dollars worth of work? If you're willing to take the risk, it will strengthen your relationships with those clients and develop trust equity in a way that is congruent with your goals of building a profitable law practice.

3.1.3 BE INTENTIONAL ABOUT THE CLIENTS YOU TAKE ... AND KEEP

There is a lawyer in town who has a solo bodily injury practice. He lists on his website fifty-nine practice areas. Fifty-nine! He is trying to reach every possible potential client who may have at some point become injured or have fallen ill at any point in their lives for any reason. What he is communicating instead is a lack of expertise in any practice area.

We all face the same problem. We want to attract as much potential business as possible. If we fail to list some practice area on your website or bio, will a potential client decide to go to a competitor instead? Yes, that's possible. But what's equally likely is that if you list all the practice areas, you will miss out on clients because they don't know what it is you specialize in.

BEING ALL THINGS TO ALL PEOPLE IS IMPRACTICAL

I faced a similar decision in the writing of this book. When I first started writing *Level Up Your Law Practice*, it would be my third book for lawyers about practice and client management (as it is now). But in between what it started as and what it has become, there was a time when this book would be for any client-facing business-person in a professional or service sector.

I workshopped titles that fit the broadened scope. The architecture of the book and topics required only minimal changes. The scope of the book really does fit many people with businesses that face clients and customers. A quick look through the chapter titles reveals as much. So what was the problem, and why did I change it (again)?

I reached out to my cover designer, who's always had good advice for me. I asked what she thought about the title and expanding the scope of the work and its intended audience. Her response about the audience really struck a chord: "As for target audience, I don't think your approach is misguided but it's a gamble. You have a chance to build a body of work that over time will dominate your professional niche vs. trying to broaden your reach to compete in other niches and then end up not reaching anybody."

I had gotten so enthralled with the idea of writing one of those business books that hits it big and sells millions of copies, that I had lost sight of my bigger goals. I am a lawyer writing for lawyers. I wasn't considering my larger body of work. Most of the non-fiction books that I still have in mind to write are for or about lawyers. Lawyers are my audience. Lawyers are the people on my mailing list. They are the folks I interact with on social media. They are my people.

I was considering sacrificing my relationship with my existing audience for my ambitions of grandeur and the (unlikely) potential of millions of book sales. Ambition isn't necessarily bad, but it should be measured. And my ambition had created a little self-absorption.

SO HOW DO WE APPLY THIS TO OUR LAW PRACTICES?

Focus your services on what you do well. Can you have fifty-nine practice areas? Maybe. But you won't be known for that. Trying to be known for your ability to do everything is much more likely to lead you to be known for nothing. Consider this observation about his business from artist and designer Nela Dunato:

> I've narrowed down and focused my services around what I do best. I used to offer many different types of design services because I've had the experience, but I've noticed a trend among my best clients — they always order logo design and branding first, and move on from there. Deciding what I'll no longer offer to new clients has helped me to streamline my on-boarding process significantly.[1]

There are two important reasons for limiting your practice areas. You provide more value to your clients by developing your expertise and skill sets in areas relevant to their needs. And you limit your competition to only those other lawyers practicing within your limited practice areas, rather than all the other firms practicing within fifty-nine different areas.

It can be difficult to cull out practice areas and intentionally limit yourself to only promoting certain lines of business. It can feel like you are intentionally cutting yourself off from potential revenue sources. But in the end that won't be the practical effect. By specializing, you will create a reputation for being an expert within a particular niche. You will receive referrals that would not otherwise have come your way. One of my partners has within the last couple of years added two corporate clients because they were looking to add panel counsel in Alabama and *other lawyers* suggested the companies should hire her because of her expertise within a particular practice area. When they reached out to her, she had the knowledge and confidence in her skills to land the business because she had self-limited and developed her expertise.

Here are some introspective questions to ask for deciding on your niche: What practice areas do you enjoy? What do you *not* want to do? Where does your experience lie? Who are your current clients and audience?

Once you know the answers to these questions, you will be better positioned to begin marketing yourself within your areas of specialization. Once I performed this analysis, I knocked four practice areas off my law firm bio and limited myself to areas that I know well and have clients that send me business in. That said, I'm open to learning new practice areas and developing my skills, but what I'm promoting to potential clients is what I know well and am known for.

LIMIT YOUR PRACTICE AREAS TO WHAT IS PROFITABLE

Not all practice areas are created equally. Some are more profitable than others. And some aren't profitable at all. When I started practicing, one of the clients I was assigned to was an insurance company whose subrogation work we did. Typically, one of their insureds (usually, a trucking company) had been involved in motor vehicle accident that wasn't the insured's fault. We were tasked with obtaining a settlement or suing on behalf of the insured and insurance company to recover for what the insurance carrier had paid out in property damage and other consequential damages.

The subrogation work was interesting and differed from much of the other work I was doing at the time. It also paid by the hour, no matter if we ultimately made a recovery.

As I got some experience, I began to market my subrogation experience and acquired some of my own clients. I joined a national organization and began to get involved with developing my subrogation practice area.

I also began to learn that our client who paid for subrogation work on a billable hour basis was in the minority. Most companies wanted to send me work on a contingency contract. After I had a half dozen of my own cases under my belt, I figured out the cases they were sending me were time consuming and the likelihood of recovery was questionable, at best. If the company could have resolved the matter on their own, they would have. But they couldn't, so they were sending it to me.

Sometimes I reached a settlement agreement with the tortfeasor. More often, I obtained an uncollectible judgment. One time, I spent more than a hundred hours on a case that we ended up voluntarily dismissing because the insured wouldn't cooperate, and we couldn't prove the case without their cooperation.

I was a young lawyer with a developing practice area. I had established some of my own clients. Things were looking promising, except for one small problem. I wasn't making any money. I had a growing practice area that wasn't profitable. I assessed the situation and decided to shutter my subrogation practice.

The work I was getting wasn't worth the time I was spending on it. Not only was it not profitable, it was taking up time that I could have been spending on other cases. On work that actually made money for the firm.

If you haven't surveyed your practice areas lately, now may be a good time to do so. If you have flat fee or contract work, is it making you money? Are there certain contingency cases that you're regularly losing money on? Maybe it's time to cut bait.

Understanding where you're profitable and what kind of work you enjoy (and hopefully there's some crossover between the two) enables you to identify practice areas you can specialize in. Bedros Keuilian, the founder and CEO of Fit Body Boot Camp, makes this recommendation: "With the array of analytic tools now at your disposal, you can constantly evaluate and tweak an aspect of your business. Pick one thing that could make your business stand out and become obsessive and relentless about growing it, optimizing, and streamlining it."[2] Having a profitable niche allows you to stand out from your competition, develop expertise, and take your law practice to the next level.

BE INTENTIONAL ABOUT THE CLIENTS YOU TAKE

Just as certain practice areas can be unprofitable, so too can particular clients. I have a friend who's fond of saying that you make just as much money off the clients you don't take as the ones you do. The clients you decline leave you room work on the work generated by your existing clients and create space to take other clients who do fit you and your practice.

A few years ago, a company approached my firm and wanted us to do their work. It was a practice area we knew well, something we were known for being particularly good at. But there was a hiccup. The company wanted us to do the work on a flat fee.

We ran the numbers and had internal discussions. The fee they were willing to pay wouldn't keep us in the black unless we settled every case early in the litigation process. In some respects, it was tempting to take on a new client that could produce a large volume of business. But when the volume is a losing proposition and you're bleeding money with every hour you work, every case hurts your bottom line.

We turned the potential client down, because it didn't align with our business interests. At its core, our business interest is to stay in business, which we can't do if we're losing money with every assignment a client sends our way.

FIRE BAD CLIENTS

When you have a client who consumes too much of your resources and you're not being adequately compensated, it's time to take an accounting of whether the client is worth the hassle. There may be outliers, but more often, the answer is that you have to shed your practice of bad clients.

Consider this from writing coach Laura Pennington: "It's never easy to let someone go, but I found that getting rid of one to three bad clients freed up my time and energy to be amazingly of service to people who were a better fit. If someone was too difficult, too demanding of my time, or simply contacting me too often, I let them go. Every few months, evaluate whether or not any of your relationships are still working of whether they are conflict-ridden or just aggravating. Up-leveling means releasing people who are no longer of service to you or who you are no longer of service to."

Your law firm is a for-profit enterprise, and you have to treat it that way. If there's an aspect of your practice that isn't profitable, whether it's a client or an entire practice area, you need to evaluate whether to keep it or let go. To borrow a sentiment from William Faulkner, you must be willing to kill your darlings if they aren't serving your goals and interests.

3.1.4 HOW EXPENDABLE ARE YOU?

A PARTNER at another firm recently said to me, "I was never the kind of associate that anyone said, 'We can't lose that guy.'" In fact, *most* associates never have that said about them. Most associates are pretty replaceable, even good associates. Good associates deliver solid work-product, meet their billable requirements, and don't make waves. But there are thousands, even tens of thousands of young lawyers who can do those things. So what do you have to do to become non-expendable, or at least the closest thing to it in the legal industry?

The answer to the question is far easier than any of the things you'll have to do to get there — *all* you have to do is develop your own business relationships. That's it. Yeah, I know. Why is that potential client you've been eyeballing going to send their business to you? In fact, we may be getting ahead of ourselves. Maybe the more pressing question is how do you find potential clients to start swooning over in the first place?

WHERE TO FIND POTENTIAL CLIENTS AND START FORMING BUSINESS RELATIONSHIPS

One of the best ways to find potential clients is to be a part of industry organizations and go to conferences. But merely being a part of the organization or going to the conference are insufficient. You can go for years just existing within those ecosystems and putting on your firm bio that you're a member of Organization X without every forming business relationships as a result.

You need to get involved. Find a way to make contributions. Write articles. Ask and answer questions in discussion forums. Join substantive law committees.

As for attending conferences, you have to establish to your firm why sending you to a conference is beneficial to them. This may require you to do some research and make a sales pitch about it. Once you get the green light to go, you should get an attendee list ahead of time so you can reach out to clients and potential clients to have dinner or just meet up. I've landed one insurance client this way and expanded business with another. If your firm isn't inclined to let you go, push for them to do it anyway. Show them there's a return on their investment. If you don't develop your own business relationships, you're doing yourself a disservice.

Here's an in-house lawyer's thoughts on the importance of attending industry conferences: "My company doesn't pay for conferences, so if I can't get comp'ed somehow, I pay out of pocket. Even in-house, going is important for the networking and career development aspect." If our clients think the networking opportunities at conferences are important, that should be a glaring signal to us.

When I was talking to one of my client's one day, I expressed that I always feel bad for the insurance folks at these big conferences because they're like the pretty girl that everyone bothers and wants to take to prom. His response was, "THAT'S WHY I GO! And to find lawyers I want to work with."

In his book *Your First 1,000 Copies*, Tim Grahl tells readers what he did in preparation for attending SXSW in Austin when he was launching his book marketing business. It fits in extraordinarily well with the point here.

> In the lead-up to the conference, I went into a frenzy researching every speaker and found every one that had ever written a book. I then began searching Twitter and the SXSW online community for anyone that worked in the publishing industry.
>
> Once I had made my list, I began contacting every one of them asking to set up a meeting during the conference. I scheduled meetings anywhere from 6: oo a.m. to 1 1: oo p.m. My hard work paid off because, when I landed in Austin the day of the conference, I had a schedule packed with people in the industry, some potential clients and others key influencers.
>
> My time at SXSW was over before I knew it. The experience was exhausting but totally worth it because I had two new clients and over a dozen new contacts by the time I got home. I had worked hard to get my business well positioned for a lot of growth within the publishing world. Those outreach efforts then continue to provide opportunities today.[1]

Be where your clients are. Create ways to meet new people once you're there. Your ability and willingness to form business relationships directly correlates with your long-term success.

AFTER YOU'VE IDENTIFIED A POTENTIAL CLIENT ...

Once you've met someone who may be interested in doing business with you, it's time to cultivate the relationship. This can be a long process. It may be months or years before they are ready to hire you as counsel. In 2019, I began receiving work from a client who I had been courting for more than a year. During that time, I had reached out from time to time. I had sent them updates on changes to Alabama law that might affect their business. Then one day, they reached out saying they needed representation in Alabama. The trust equity that I had been cultivating by sharing useful information with them without always asking them to hire me led me to earn their business.

I do not use term "relationship" flippantly. Business relationships share the same foundational principles as personal relationships. Before your potential client will commit to doing business with you, you have to establish (at a minimum) that you understand their business, you are trustworthy, and you have the expertise necessary to guide them to a successful result.

If you don't build trust equity and lay the foundations for the relationship before you ask for a commitment, things can get weird.

A couple of years ago, I was at an insurance defense conference where I and other lawyers went to dinner with some potential new clients. We had a nice meal. We talked about the business in various states where the potential clients had work. The lawyers talked about their firms and the kind of work they did. That was the purpose of this meeting — to get to know each other, see if we liked each other, and if down the road we could do business together. It was basically a first date for business folks.

But one of the lawyers got a little handsy at the end of the meal (figuratively speaking). He began to push the potential new client to make a commitment to use his firm as their panel counsel in his state. He wasn't just forward; he was persistent.

For the spectators, it was uncomfortable watching this unravel. It was also evident that the potential new client found it off-putting and was no longer a potential new client. The formerly potential client was trying to disengage and wrap up dinner. The date had gone wrong. It wasn't a good match. And the only person who didn't know it was the overly aggressive lawyer.

The problem was that they didn't have a relationship yet. He hadn't built trust equity or established his expertise. He hadn't done anything to establish that he was able to do the work the potential client required. Yet he was asking for a commitment.

The strategy was inappropriate and ineffective. It's also too common among lawyers courting new business. Many lawyers approach potential clients this way. I myself have done it. But it is no way to operate and no way to establish good relationships with people with whom you want to do business.

PEOPLE DO BUSINESS WITH THOSE THEY KNOW, LIKE, AND TRUST

There is an axiom that "people do business with people they know, like, and trust." The way to get someone from a contact to a new client is by "building lifetime relationships on trust, creating value, collaborating, and delivering exceptional results."[2] To accomplish this, you have to understand the challenges your would-be client is facing and try to help them solve their problems.[3]

You're getting the order wrong if you are asking your contacts for something before providing any value to them. To create the transition in your relationship, you must create a "relationship of value" in which "you create value for your clients as someone who provides ideas and advice — and who also ensures that the outcomes they sell are delivered."[4] You have to be others-minded and engage your empathy.

This is what I have been calling trust equity. And it is the currency that will enable you to begin developing your own business. The medium by which you will go from expendable to indispensable. But the transition takes time. Building a book of business is a career effort. It takes persistence and not a little bit of luck. By *luck* I mean doing the work that puts you in the right place at the right time.

Thomas Jefferson is quoted as saying, "I am a great believer in luck, and I find the harder I work, the more I have of it." So don't be afraid to put in the work. Build your business relationships as if your career depends on it.

3.2 WHAT TO DO WITH CLIENTS' ATTENTION

3.2.1 SET YOUR CLIENTS' EXPECTATIONS EARLY

WHAT DO your clients expect from your relationship? Are their expectations based on what you've communicated to them? Or have they set their own expectations because you haven't filled that void? If it's the latter, that's a dangerous place to be.

To fully be in charge of the client relationship and to create a situation in which clients are most likely to be satisfied with their experience with you, you must tell them what to expect. They need to understand the process, timelines, and how you go about things. Entrepreneur Paul Jarvis has compared failing to set client expectations with "jumping out a window and hoping it's not the 27th floor."[1]

Expectations should be set early and in writing. You can do this either formally in a memorandum of understanding that you and the client sign, or more informally in a client representation letter. The importance of it being in writing is so there is no variance and no valid claim for misunderstanding later during the representation. You should not only outline expectations in the beginning but also deliver on them.[2]

If *you* aren't the one setting expectations, the client will be. Their expectations will be self-serving and not aligned with your processes or intentions. And they will expect more of you than you are prepared to give. Allowing clients to create their own expectations sets the tone from the outset for you ceding control of the relationship. This will eventually lead to disappointment and a fractured relationship.

Below are several steps that will enable you to set your clients' expectations and build a foundation for a successful relationship.

EDUCATE YOUR CLIENT ABOUT WHAT TO EXPECT FROM YOU

The key is that you are giving clients a full understanding of what they're getting into and how it's going to work. Tripp Watson of The Watson Firm has an article on his firm website that he directs clients to called "What to Expect Working with Me." It reads in part: "When people set foot in a lawyer's office, they are often given a multi-page contract and told to sign the agreement before they have had a chance to review the terms. While we still use a written agreement, we publicly post our requirements for you and your expectations of working with us. I do this to prevent any surprise you might have when you receive the agreement."[3]

Watson outlines the scope of his representation, his communication methods, the firm's "five-minute rule" about whether a phone call or email will be billed, and his standard rates, and after-hours rates. By providing this information on his website (and discussing it again in person during the initial consultation), he educates the client from the outset about what to expect from the relationship.

Having your parameters in writing also keep you accountable to the client. Sharing processes and timelines for when you will get things done is great to keep you on track and will keep your clients' expectations in check.[4]

UNDERSTAND THEIR GOALS IN RETAINING YOU

If you are not thoroughly listening to your clients' problems and the reasons they're seeking to hire you, you will be unable to properly set their expectations for how the matter will resolve. Setting expectations starts with asking the client what they're hoping to achieve and exhausting that line of discussion. While initial phone calls can be beneficial, you can enhance expectation setting with in-person visits where you can develop a closer connection and have a more meaningful dialogue with the client.[5] The purpose is to obtain a fuller understanding of what the client is focusing on, which will help you recognize their need and how you can help them reach an outcome they see as successful.[6]

DISCUSS COMMUNICATION METHODS AND TIMING

Early on, discuss with clients preferences between calls or emails, in-person meetings or quick reports, and be clear about how you work best and how they work best. This collaborative communication approach will help your relationship be more successful. After establishing these preferences, reach out to the client with sufficient regularity to stay on top of expectations and perspectives about how the relationship is going.[7]

Merrianne Dean has provided a good example of how client education about communication methods and timing is important. If she didn't communicate with her clients that she only checks email twice daily, there would be some shock factor when they receive the first auto-responder from her. But Dean sets not only that expectation early, but also informs clients about her availability more generally.

Here's a refresher: "Another aspect of controlling your work environment is to make sure clients and opposing counsel know that you are NOT available evenings and weekends. I've declined work when the client insists on being able to communicate 24/7. Really, there is nothing I can do outside of regular business hours that will benefit my clients or their cases that isn't better done during regular business hours." Both her methods and time are established from the outset, with little room for misunderstanding

OUTLINE YOUR EXPECTATIONS FOR YOUR CLIENT

Not only do you need to establish boundaries for what clients can expect from you, you must also communicate your expectations for them. That includes not only responding to communications and the timing of paying invoices, but also for honesty and forthrightness. I regularly tell my clients, "I'm the guy you tell everything to. No matter how bad it is. Because I can't tell anyone else and I can't help you if I get surprised with something down the road that you were hiding." But as you already know, I still get surprised with things down the road that they had not chosen to share.

You have to establish parameters at the outset. And you must enforce them. If the client no-shows or cancels a meeting at the last minute and your contract says there's a charge for it, charge them. Giving clients a pass encourages the wrong behavior and gives them license to do it again.[8] Your time is valuable and finite. Any time you set aside to help that client is time that you unable to work for other clients.

PROVIDE REGULAR UPDATES THROUGHOUT THE REPRESENTATION

If you work for corporate clients who regularly work with lawyers, you likely have reporting schedules that you have to comply with. If instead you're working with people who don't have reporting systems in place, you may have to develop your own protocols. Regular updates to clients are critical to the communication process: "Status reports not only help assure clients that their time (and, effectively, their money) is not going to waste. They also keep you honest and realistic about your timelines, work, and budgets."[9] They also keep clients from badgering you about what's going on with their case. They know when they're going to hear from you and what form that communication will take.

On the other hand, if the only written communication your clients are receiving from you is your monthly invoice, they will develop seeds of doubt. Status reports build trust and keep clients informed about their case. They provide you an expected channel in which you can share both good and bad news. Transparent and consistent communication forms a bond, and helps create a foundation of trust for lasting relationships.[10]

PERFORM AUDITS TO MAKE SURE YOU'RE DELIVERING ON EXPECTATIONS YOU SET

Earlier in the book, I wrote about the importance of focusing on processes, not outcomes. Ensuring that you're delivering on the expectations you set for your clients is a process you need to audit for compliance. You should identify if there are gaps between what you're claiming you will do in your practice and what you are actually delivering.[11]

One way I do this is by keeping a spreadsheet that monitors the status of each of my litigation files.[12] Most of my clients have reporting guidelines with specific timelines that are triggered at different stages of the case – 30 days after the assignment, after party depositions, before mediation, and 45 days before trial. By keeping track of these timelines with a spreadsheet, I can self-monitor for how effectively I am delivering on the expectations the client has for my reporting about the case.

THE MOST IMPORTANT THING ABOUT EXPECTATIONS

Here's the thing about expectations in the context of a client relationship — expectations are going to exist. You can either be the person to set them and thereby control the direction of the relationship. Or you can neglect to do so and have them foisted upon you. In doing so, you cede control of the relationship and set it up for failure and disappointment.

Bill Watterson, the creator of *Calvin and Hobbes*, once said, "I find my life is a lot easier the lower I keep my expectations." This is not the attitude you want your clients to have toward you — they find their life a lot easier the lower they keep their expectations for you. But it is exactly what will happen if you omit telling them what to expect from you and the business you're handling for them. They will set a threshold for success that you are unable to cross.

Set client expectations early. Affirm them as often as necessary. And rely on the communication and case management processes you have created to get you and your client to the outcome you have outlined for them.

3.2.2 ESTABLISH YOUR PRIORITIES
FOR CLIENT RELATIONSHIPS

MOST OF MY clients are insurance companies and corporate entities that deal with lawyers and the litigation process all the time. The scope of what I want to communicate to them early on may differ from someone who works with small business owners and individuals who may not regularly or ever have previously worked with a lawyer.

What I want clients to know is what I emphasize and how I prefer to work collaboratively for us to manage the litigation process in a way that meets their needs. Here's how I communicate that on our firm website:

"When approaching cases, my priority is to collaborate with clients to achieve efficient and effective results by way of tenacious advocacy. I strive to align my tactics and objectives with my client's goals in handling cases. I enjoy the various aspects of litigation, ranging from strategy and planning that go into research and brief writing, to the in-person chess matches that take place during depositions and trial. It is important to me to keep my clients and myself informed of trends and developments in Alabama law so we can most effectively evaluate and prosecute cases to the best possible result."

When I'm pitching to new clients talking about the importance of collaboration and open communication lines, they may think it's so much fluff. They regularly get presentations from lawyers in which they're getting told what lawyers think the potential client wants to hear. But if they go check out my website bio, they'll see collaboration and communication is something I am serious about it. It's a topic I speak about at conferences and write articles about – more evidence of the importance of content marketing. They will find that having a collaborative relationship is truly one of my priorities.

There are other things I prioritize as well: compliance with reporting guidelines, evaluating cases for risk and potential settlement as early in the process as possible, and providing accurate litigation budgets. These things are important to me because they are important to my clients. These priorities communicate to the potential client that I understand their needs and can meet these needs.

In his book *Building a StoryBrand*, Donald Miller writes that it is necessary for business owners to identify clients' problems for them and establish that they can guide the client to a solution. We have to communicate a message to the client that gives them confidence that we will improve their situation. "'The customer simply needs to know that you have something they want and you can be trusted to deliver whatever that is."[1]

Establishing your priorities isn't just in the broader communications strategies you will implement. It's also about establishing tactics you will (and won't) use to resolve your clients' problems.

If your practice differs from mine, your priorities likely will too. Make sure you've internally identified your client relation-

ship priorities so that during pitching meetings or initial consul-
tations, you can establish them with your potential client. This
will allow you to distinguish yourself from the competition and
create a workflow that incorporates your priorities.

3.2.3 COMMUNICATE LIKE YOUR LIVELIHOOD DEPENDS ON IT

I REMAIN impressed (and not in a good way) with lawyers who fail to emphasize effective and timely communication with clients. They are so busy with the seeming urgency of managing their caseloads that they aren't doing the important work of maintaining their relationships with their clients.

When clients feel neglected, even if you are competently doing their work, they're eventually going to either start openly looking for another lawyer or be receptive to someone else's advances. And make no mistake, there are always other lawyers waiting to move in on your clients.

TIMELY COMMUNICATION IS IMPORTANT

An in-house lawyer made these comments on Twitter about the importance of communication with clients:

> While certainly not all, there is a large portion of firm lawyers that don't seem to realize how many other firms exist out there, doing the same work they do. Lawyers that don't

make an effort, don't try to learn about my business, don't respond timely, etc., are putting themselves at a significant disadvantage for repeat business. Making me feel stupid or acting like I'm not worth your time is not going to end well.

This is something I think about whenever I have to use certain counsel for reasons beyond my control.

And conversely, the counsel that I go back to again and again are the ones that have taken the time to learn about my business, the politics at play, and make an effort to always respond, even if the response is just, "I'm slammed but will get back to you."

A new business client called me a few weeks ago. They had an urgent problem. We needed to get all their things in order and prepare to have suit filed within the next two weeks. We were exchanging emails and phone calls at all hours. The client and I went from total strangers to pretty well acquainted within a short span of time.

One of the things they said to me early in the process was this: "We really appreciate how responsive you've been. That ... hasn't been our experience with other firms in your state."

At some point it will no longer surprise me that so many lawyers don't choose to provide timely communication with and for clients. But today is not that day.

Part of the problems is that we do not see ourselves as a service industry. But we absolutely are. We exchange our time and expertise for our client's money. But if we don't meet their needs, of which communication is one of the primary components, they will find someone else to handle their problems.

Recognize that your clients need to hear from you. When they call or email, you should make a point to respond promptly, even when things are crazy. I was trained to respond within 24 hours, even if that's just to say, "I got your message.

I'll get back to you soon." That affirmation, even though not a substantive response, tells the client that you have heard them and allows them to infer their value.

When your clients believe that you value them and when they receive regular, timely communication from you, they will remain loyal to you and continue to send you work. Assuming of course that your work product is equally good.

3.2.4 YOUR CLIENTS HAVE CHOICES, BE THEIRS

YOUR CLIENTS HAVE CHOICES. I've given you some tools that will help you continue to be your clients' choice. But there's also some bad news: several things are working against you forming and maintaining life-long relationships with your clients.

Your clients have never had more options for hungry lawyers than they do now. It has never been easier for your clients to find a new lawyer. People aren't brand loyal like they have been in the past; a 2019 study performed by Neilsen revealed that only 9% of consumers in the United States consider themselves to be brand loyal.[1]

At the same time, only 36% of people said they love trying new brands and products.[2] One way to interpret that data is that 64% don't particularly want to change brands but are willing to if given a reason. They know they have plenty of options, but they are willing to stick with what they know and are comfortable with as long as doing so makes sense. Your clients have choices about where to send their work. Give them reasons to send it to you.

Client relationships are like any other relationships. They require trust, understanding, and communication. Your clients have needs that you need to be cognizant of. By recognizing your clients' needs, meeting those needs, and then communicating with the client about it, you are building trust and forming a bond. You are giving your clients reasons to stick with you and not look around at their many other options.

Your ability to level-up your law practice rests in large part on your ability to retain desirable clients. Having regular clients means dependable income. Happy clients can also be an important source of word-of-mouth marketing. Additionally, prioritizing your clients just like other successful businesses do in other service sectors encourages repeat business. Several other keys to client satisfaction are "asking for and acting on feedback, addressing issues and complaints quickly and thoroughly, and being consistently accessible and accountable."[3]

A failure to prioritize your clients will result in unhappy clients. A client who believes his correspondence or phone calls are going into an abyss is a discontent client. A client whose expectations aren't being met will be unhappy about it. And unhappy clients don't stick around. Even if they're among the 64% who don't want to hop from one brand to another. Dissatisfaction will drive them into the open arms of one of your competitors. You will experience a shrinking client base, decreased profits, and bad word-of-mouth.

Micah Solomon contends that client satisfaction can be broken down into four factors. Your clients will be satisfied when they consistently receive: (1) service that performs as expected within established boundaries; (2) service that is delivered by an empathetic person; (3) service that is performed in a timely fashion; and (4) service that effectively resolves their problem.[4] If you can achieve these things regularly, you will be on your way not only to satisfied clients but to loyal clients.

Your law practice is alive because of your clients. The better you can understand their needs, the better you can meet them. Client engagement and communication has to be as much a priority to us as complying with scheduling orders and other deadlines. Because without clients, we don't need to worry about any of the rest of it.

If you need any motivation, just remember that only 9% of people consider themselves to be brand loyal. The other 91% are free agents. And it's never been easier for those free agents to find another lawyer. Give them every reason not to go looking. Your clients have plenty of choices — be theirs.

IT'S TIME TO GO AFTER BOWSER

YOU COULD LOOK at this as saving Princess Peach. But I always found the idea of slaying Bowser much more compelling than saving Peach. I don't know what that says about me. But I digress.

You've got some tools for getting your mindset in order. For getting out of your own way and refusing to place false limitations on yourself. You understand the importance of an abundance mindset in which you believe there's always more where that came from. You have some defensive measures in place that protect you from the onslaught of daily life.

But you've also got fireballs. You get to go on the offensive. You get to be ambitious and dream about the law practice you want. Dream big. Because with S.M.A.R.T. goals and key performance indicators, you can monitor the progress you're making and adjust as needed.

And clients. Let's not forget them. Without clients, you don't get to practice law; you just get to call yourself a lawyer. So make sure to go where the clients are. Make yourself and your firm discoverable. And treat your clients like the stars they are.

With these tools and ideas, you should feel empowered. Both personally and professionally. I hope you are encouraged and ready to take on new ventures. Whether you prefer to see those ventures as saving Princess Peach or taking down Bowser, I wish you the best of luck as you take your law practice to the next level.

LEAVE A REVIEW

IF YOU ENJOYED *Level Up Your Law Practice*, please leave a review on either Amazon or Goodreads. Reviews are lifeblood for authors and encourage others to read good books.

ABOUT THE AUTHOR

Jeremy W. Richter practices civil defense litigation in Birmingham, Alabama. He discovered early in his practice that managing cases is only half the battle in the practice of law. Building and maintaining relationships with clients is equally important. Jeremy has set out to innovate ways to develop client relationships and improve methods for achieving efficient and effective results.

This is his third book, in which he chronicles his efforts and lessons learned along the way to becoming a better lawyer. His first two books are *Building a Better Law Practice* and *Stop Putting Out Fires*.

Jeremy also writes a law blog at jeremywrichter.com.

NOTES

INTRODUCTION

1. Ken Brokaw, "Leveling Up Life and Business," https://www.huffpost.com/entry/leveling-up-life-and-business-how-to-become-your-own_b_59edf44be4b034105edd5047.

IN NEED OF A MUSHROOM

1. William Shakespeare, *Hamlet*, Act III, Scene 1.

1.1.1 CULTIVATE AN ABUNDANCE MINDSET

1. Tony Robbins on "The School of Greatness" Podcast, Episode 109.
2. Michael Hyatt, "Want an Abundant Life? Change Your Thinking: 8 Reasons Why You Shouldn't Be Scared by Scarcity," https://michaelhyatt.com/change-your-thinking/.
3. Shahram Heshmat, "The Scarcity Mindset," https://www.psychologytoday.com/us/blog/science-choice/201504/the-scarcity-mindset.
4. We'll talk more about the importance of client communication in the chapter, "Communicate Like Your Livelihood Depends on It."
5. Alice Boyes, "How to Focus on What's Important, Not Just What's Urgent," https://hbr.org/2018/07/how-to-focus-on-whats-important-not-just-whats-urgent.
6. You can learn more about my case management spreadsheets in *Building a Better Law Practice*.
7. Alice Boyes, "How to Focus on What's Important, Not Just What's Urgent," https://hbr.org/2018/07/how-to-focus-on-whats-important-not-just-whats-urgent.

1.1.2 MINIMIZE SELF-LIMITING BELIEFS

1. Andrew Blackman, "What Are Self-Limiting Beliefs? + How to Overcome

Them Successfully," https://business.tutsplus.com/tutorials/what-are-self-limiting-beliefs--cms-31607.

2. Andrew Blackman, "What Are Self-Limiting Beliefs? + How to Overcome Them Successfully," https://business.tutsplus.com/tutorials/what-are-self-limiting-beliefs--cms-31607.

3. Amy Morin, "3 Types of Self-Limiting Beliefs That Will Keep You Stuck in Life (and What to Do About Them)," https://www.inc.com/amy-morin/3-types-of-unhealthy-beliefs-that-will-drain-your-mental-strength-make-you-less-effective.html.

4. Gwen Moran, "5 Habits to Get Over Self-Limiting Beliefs," https://www.fastcompany.com/3058647/5-habits-to-get-over-self-limiting-beliefs.

5. Joanna Penn, *The Successful Author Mindset: A Handbook for Surviving the Writer's Journey*, p. 22 (Kindle Edition).

6. Gwen Moran, "5 Habits to Get Over Self-Limiting Beliefs," https://www.fastcompany.com/3058647/5-habits-to-get-over-self-limiting-beliefs.

7. Michael Hyatt, "Are Your Beliefs Keeping You Stuck?" https://michaelhyatt.com/limiting-beliefs/.

8. Andrew Blackman, "What Are Self-Limiting Beliefs? +How to Overcome Them Successfully," https://business.tutsplus.com/tutorials/what-are-self-limiting-beliefs--cms-31607.

9. Andrew Blackman, "What Are Self-Limiting Beliefs? + How to Overcome Them Successfully," https://business.tutsplus.com/tutorials/what-are-self-limiting-beliefs--cms-31607.

10. Andrew Blackman, "What Are Self-Limiting Beliefs? + How to Overcome Them Successfully," https://business.tutsplus.com/tutorials/what-are-self-limiting-beliefs--cms-31607.

11. Gwen Moran, "5 Habits to Get Over Self-Limiting Beliefs," https://www.fastcompany.com/3058647/5-habits-to-get-over-self-limiting-beliefs.

1.1.3 APPLY HEALTHY MOTIVATORS

1. Note: It was not a great business idea.

2. The Enneagram Institute, "Enneagram Type Three: The Achiever," https://www.enneagraminstitute.com/type-3.

3. The Enneagram Institute, "Enneagram Type Three: The Achiever," https://www.enneagraminstitute.com/type-3.

4. Bill M. Hours, "On the Virtue of Spite Cookies," *Six Minutes to Kill*, http://sixminutestokill.com/blog/on-the-virtue-of-spite-cookies.

5. Alan Morris, "Positive Motivation vs. Negative Motivation: Which One Works Better?" https://addicted2success.com/motivation/positive-motivation-vs-negative-motivation-which-one-works-better/.

6. Eric O'Flaherty (@EOF34), https://twitter.com/EOF34/status/1212000549479927808 [Dec. 31, 2019].

7. Joanne Harris (@joannechocalat), https://twitter.com/Joannechocolat/status/1211685642582872064 [Dec. 30, 2019].

8. Joanne Harris (@joannechocolat), https://twitter.com/Joannechocolat/status/1211239346273243136 [Dec. 29, 2019].

1.1.4 AVOID COMPARISONITIS

1. *Holy Bible*, Genesis 3:1-6.
2. "Envy," https://www.goodtherapy.org/blog/psychpedia/envy.
3. Joanna Penn, *The Successful Author Mindset: A Handbook for Surviving the Writer's Journey*, p. 67 (Kindle Edition).
4. Dr. Neel Burton, "The Psychology and Philosophy of Envy," https://www.psychologytoday.com/us/blog/hide-and-seek/201408/the-psychology-and-philosophy-envy.

1.2.1 MANAGE YOUR FEAR OF FAILURE

1. Tchiki Davis, "Three Ways to Overcome Fear of Failure at Work," *Greater Good Magazine*, https://greatergood.berkeley.edu/article/item/three_ways_to_overcome_fear_of_failure_at_work.
2. "Overcoming Fear of Failure: Facing Your Fear of Moving Forward," https://www.mindtools.com/pages/article/fear-of-failure.htm.
3. Susan Peppercorn, "How to Overcome Your Fear of Failure," *Harvard Business Review*, https://hbr.org/2018/12/how-to-overcome-your-fear-of-failure.
4. Lahcen Haddad, "Seeing Failure as an Opportunity to Learn From (and Leapfrog into Success)," https://www.entrepreneur.com/article/308943.
5. Tchiki Davis, "Three Ways to Overcome Fear of Failure at Work," Greater Good Magazine, https://greatergood.berkeley.edu/article/item/three_ways_to_overcome_fear_of_failure_at_work.
6. Susan Tardanico, "Five Ways to Make Peace with Failure," *Forbes*, https://www.forbes.com/sites/susantardanico/2012/09/27/five-ways-to-make-peace-with-failure/#16628b9c3640.
7. Andrew Blackman, "What Are Self-Limiting Beliefs? +How to Overcome Them Successfully," https://business.tutsplus.com/tutorials/what-are-self-limiting-beliefs--cms-31607.
8. Vanessa Loder, "How To Conquer The Fear Of Failure - 5 Proven Strategies," https://www.forbes.com/sites/vanessaloder/2014/10/30/how-to-move-beyond-the-fear-of-failure-5-proven-strategies/#58d48c071b78.
9. Jon Simmons, "Here are 3 ways to overcome fear of failure in your career," https://www.monster.com/career-advice/article/ways-to-overcome-fear-of-failure-in-career.
10. Vanessa Loder, "How To Conquer The Fear Of Failure - 5 Proven Strategies," https://www.forbes.com/sites/vanessaloder/2014/10/30/how-to-move-beyond-the-fear-of-failure-5-proven-strategies/#58d48c071b78.
11. Theo Tsaousides, "How to Conquer Fear of Failure," Psychology Today,

https://www.psychologytoday.com/us/blog/smashing-the-brainblocks/
201801/how-conquer-fear-failure.

12. Tchiki Davis, "Three Ways to Overcome Fear of Failure at Work," Greater
Good Magazine, https://greatergood.berkeley.edu/article/
item/three_ways_to_overcome_fear_of_failure_at_work.

13. Elyse Santilli, "10 Ways to Cope With Stress and Overwhelm," https://
www.huffpost.com/entry/10-ways-to-cope-with-stress-and-
overwhelm_b_6033802?guccounter=1&guce_referrer=
aHR0cHM6Ly93d3cuZ29vZ2xlLmNvbS8&guce_referrer_sig=
AQAAACqe16s8Lm6Sq_tswgSBJr4h1OTgVMS1Ms-
kLAtatqn5CmlKaHtQp5vg15OWJioQtdddCTihofIfTvwdvDjY4uEjQr
RZuJotvUpW8iW8KOO8fnKodqBgS3sBztRvTFMDfnKxLEojcCxElu
YuzHulbtdiJXxNg27Dhpoc7l-Qm2Lo.

1.2.3 CRITICAL FEEDBACK OR MEAN-SPIRITED CRITICISM?

1. Business Dictionary, "Constructive Criticism," http://www.
businessdictionary.com/definition/constructive-criticism.html.

2. Joanna Penn, "Writing and the Fear of Rejection and Criticism," https://
www.thecreativepenn.com/rejection-and-criticism/.

3. United States Office of Personnel Management, "Performance Management," https://www.opm.gov.

4. "Level Up Your Business," https://beckymollenkamp.com/level-up-
advice/.

5. Joanna Penn, *The Successful Author Mindset: A Handbook for Surviving
the Writer's Journey*, p. 119-120 (Kindle Edition).

1.2.4 RESPOND APPROPRIATELY TO FEEDBACK

1. ASU CareerWise, "Receiving and Responding to Feedback," https://
careerwise.asu.edu/?q=learning-skills/communication-skills/receiving-
and-responding-to-feedback.

2. Tasha Eurich, "The Right Way to Respond to Negative Feedback, *Harvard
Business Review*, https://hbr.org/2018/05/the-right-way-to-respond-to-
negative-feedback.

3. Tasha Eurich, "The Right Way to Respond to Negative Feedback, *Harvard
Business Review*, https://hbr.org/2018/05/the-right-way-to-respond-to-
negative-feedback.

4. Tasha Eurich, "The Right Way to Respond to Negative Feedback, *Harvard
Business Review*, https://hbr.org/2018/05/the-right-way-to-respond-to-
negative-feedback.

5. "Behave Yourself," *Harvard Business Review*, https://hbr.org/2002/10/behave-yourself-2.
6. Francesca Gino, "Research: We Drop the People Who Give Us Critical Feedback," *Harvard Business Review*, https://hbr.org/2016/09/research-we-drop-people-who-give-us-critical-feedback.
7. Francesca Gino, "Research: We Drop the People Who Give Us Critical Feedback," *Harvard Business Review*, https://hbr.org/2016/09/research-we-drop-people-who-give-us-critical-feedback.
8. ASU CareerWise, "Receiving and Responding to Feedback," https://careerwise.asu.edu/?q=learning-skills/communication-skills/receiving-and-responding-to-feedback.

1.3.1 DON'T SACRIFICE YOUR CREATIVITY TO YOUR LAW PRACTICE

1. Crawford Ifland, "Why I Sell Myself 1 Hour of Time Each and Every Day," https://medium.com/the-mission/why-i-sell-myself-1-hour-of-time-each-and-every-day-80a3f20f08c2.
2. "Level Up Your Business," https://beckymollenkamp.com/level-up-advice/.
3. Alice Shroeder, *The Snowball: Warren Buffett and the Business of Life*.
4. Jay Harrington, "Sell Yourself One Hour of Your Time Every Day," *Attorney at Work*, https://www.attorneyatwork.com/eisenhower-sell-yourself-one-hour-every-day/.
5. Shane Parrish, "The Warren Buffett formula: How you can get smarter," *The Week*, https://theweek.com/articles/460783/warren-buffett-formula-how-smarter.

1.3.2 COPE BETTER WITH BEING OVERWHELMED

1. Jessica DuBois-Maahs, "How to Manage When We Feel Overwhelmed," https://www.talkspace.com/blog/feeling-overwhelmed/.
2. Rachel Gillett, "A new study shows saving your vacation time can do more harm than good," *Business Insider*, https://www.businessinsider.com/consequence-of-not-taking-vacation-2015-7 (July 15, 2015).
3. Elyse Santilli, "10 Ways to Cope With Stress and Overwhelm," https://www.huffpost.com/entry/10-ways-to-cope-with-stress-and-overwhelm_b_6033802?guccounter=1&guce_referrer=aHR0cHM6Ly93d3cuZ29vZ2xlLmNvbS8&guce_referrer_sig=AQAAACqe16s8Lm6Sq_tswgSBJr4h1OTgVMS1Ms-kLAtatqn5CmlKaHtQp5vg15OWJioQtdddCTihofIfTvwdvDjY4uEjQrRZuJotvUpW8iW8KOO8fnKodqBgS3sBztRvTFMDfnKxLE0jcCxEluYuzHulbtdiJXxNg27Dhp0c7l-Qm2L0.

4. Elyse Santilli, "10 Ways to Cope With Stress and Overwhelm," https://
www.huffpost.com/entry/10-ways-to-cope-with-stress-and-
overwhelm_b_6033802?guccounter=1&guce_referrer=
aHRocHM6Ly93d3cuZ29vZ2xlLmNvbS88&guce_referrer_sig=
AQAAACqe16s8Lm6Sq_tswgSBJr4h1OTgVMS1Ms-
kLAtatqn5CmlKaHtQp5vg15OWJioQtdddCTihofIfTvwdvDjY4uEjQr
RZuJotvUpW8iW8KOO8fnKodqBgS3sBztRvTFMDfnKxLEojcCxElu
YuzHulbtdiJXxNg27Dhpoc7l-Qm2Lo.
5. Judith Orloff, "The Secret to Managing Being Overwhelmed," https://
www.psychologytoday.com/us/blog/emotional-freedom/201610/the-
secret-managing-being-overwhelmed.

1.3.3 MAINTAIN A FUNCTIONAL WORK-LIFE IMBALANCE

1. Linsey Knerl, "6 Ways to Level Up Your Business in 2019," https://www.
nav.com/blog/6-ways-to-level-up-your-business-in-2019-33452/.
2. Angela Doucette, "Level Up Your Business," https://beckymollenkamp.
com/level-up-advice/.
3. Bedros Keuilian, "How to Level Up Your Business and Unlock Success,"
https://www.entrepreneur.com/article/327304.
4. Elyse Santilli, "10 Ways to Cope With Stress and Overwhelm," https://
www.huffpost.com/entry/10-ways-to-cope-with-stress-and-
overwhelm_b_6033802?guccounter=1&guce_referrer=
aHRocHM6Ly93d3cuZ29vZ2xlLmNvbS88&guce_referrer_sig=
AQAAACqe16s8Lm6Sq_tswgSBJr4h1OTgVMS1Ms-
kLAtatqn5CmlKaHtQp5vg15OWJioQtdddCTihofIfTvwdvDjY4uEjQr
RZuJotvUpW8iW8KOO8fnKodqBgS3sBztRvTFMDfnKxLEojcCxElu
YuzHulbtdiJXxNg27Dhpoc7l-Qm2Lo.
5. Chris Myers, "4 Coping Strategies You Can Use When You're Feeling
Overwhelmed At Work," https://www.forbes.com/sites/chrismyers/2018/
07/12/4-coping-strategies-you-can-use-when-youre-feeling-overwhelmed-
at-work/#20632579718c.

2.1.1 DEVELOP A VISION FOR YOUR LAW PRACTICE

1. Melissa Hall, "Smol Law," https://www.smol-law.com/.
2. Tripp Watson, "Mission," https://trippwatson.com/about-u.
3. Arne Giske, "Level Up Your Business," https://beckymollenkamp.com/
level-up-advice/.

2.1.2 FOCUS ON PROCESSES, NOT OUTCOMES

1. Matt Johnson, "Bill Belichick drops 'trust the process' line during presser," https://www.msn.com/en-us/sports/nfl/bill-belichick-drops-%E2%80%98trust-the-process%E2%80%99-line-during-presser/ar-BBLsFpt.
2. Max Rappaport, "The Definitive History of 'Trust the Process,'" https://bleacherreport.com/articles/2729018-the-definitive-history-of-trust-the-process.
3. "Level Up Your Business," https://beckymollenkamp.com/level-up-advice/.
4. "Sticktoitiveness" is a totally fabricated word that coaches use, which seems appropriate with all the sports analogies in this chapter.

2.1.3 DEFINE WHAT SUCCESS MEANS FOR YOU

1. Joanna Penn, *The Successful Author Mindset: A Handbook for Surviving the Writer's Journey*, p. 77-78 (Kindle Edition).

2.2.1 THE IMPORTANCE OF GOAL-SETTING

1. Alyssa Gregory, "7 Ways to Take Your Small Business to the Next Level," https://www.thebalancesmb.com/small-business-next-level-2951535.
2. University of Virginia Human Resources, "Performance Management," https://hr.virginia.edu/career-development/performance-management.
3. "Level Up Your Business," https://beckymollenkamp.com/level-up-advice/.
4. Bedros Keuilian, "How to Level Up Your Business and Unlock Success," https://www.entrepreneur.com/article/327304.
5. Peter Economy, "This Is the Way You Need to Write Down Your Goals for Faster Success," https://www.inc.com/peter-economy/this-is-way-you-need-to-write-down-your-goals-for-faster-success.html.

2.2.2 MONITOR GOALS WITH KEY PERFORMANCE INDICATORS

1. "Performance Management and KPIs," https://www.mindtools.com/pages/article/newTMM_87.htm.
2. "Performance Management and KPIs," https://www.mindtools.com/pages/article/newTMM_87.htm.
3. "What Is a Key Performance Indicator?" https://www.klipfolio.com/resources/articles/what-is-a-key-performance-indicator.

4. "Performance Management and KPIs," https://www.mindtools.com/pages/article/newTMM_87.htm.

2.3.1 DO WHAT YOU MUST AND DELEGATE
THE REST

1. Bedros Keuilian, "How to Level Up Your Business and Unlock Success," https://www.entrepreneur.com/article/327304.
2. Becky Mollenkamp, "Level Up Your Business," https://beckymollenkamp.com/level-up-advice/.
3. Alyssa Gregory, "7 Ways to Take Your Small Business to the Next Level," https://www.thebalancesmb.com/small-business-next-level-2951535.

2.3.2 BATCH YOUR PROCESSES TO WORK MORE
EFFICIENTLY

1. Faria Sana, Tina Weston, and Nicholas J. Cepeda, "Laptop multitasking hinders classroom learning for both users and nearby peers," *Science Direct*, https://www.sciencedirect.com/science/article/pii/S0360131512002254?via%3Dihub.

THAT STAR POWER

1. Jeff Goins, "The Secret to Innovative Work: Be Different, Not Better," *The Portfolio Life* (Nov. 6, 2019).

3.1.1 HELP POTENTIAL CLIENTS FIND YOU

1. Conversion Guru, "90% of people don't go past page 1 of the Google Search results when searching for you," https://www.conversionguru.co.za/2017/05/29/90-people-dont-go-past-page-1-google-search-results-searching/.
2. "7 Strategies To Take Your Business To The Next Level & Make More Money," https://www.bluchic.com/business-strategies/.
3. "Level Up Your Business," https://beckymollenkamp.com/level-up-advice/.

3.1.3 BE INTENTIONAL ABOUT THE CLIENTS YOU
TAKE ... AND KEEP

1. "Level Up Your Business," https://beckymollenkamp.com/level-up-advice/.
2. Bedros Keuilian, "How to Level Up Your Business and Unlock Success," https://www.entrepreneur.com/article/327304.

3.1.4 HOW EXPENDABLE ARE YOU?

1. Tim Grahl, *Your First 1,000 Copies*, Kindle Loc. 1014.
2. Anthony Iannarino, *The Lost Art of Closing: Winning the Ten Commitments that Drive Sales*, p. 7.
3. Anthony Iannarino, *The Lost Art of Closing: Winning the Ten Commitments that Drive Sales*, p. 5.
4. Anthony Iannarino, *The Lost Art of Closing: Winning the Ten Commitments that Drive Sales*, p. 21.

3.2.1 SET YOUR CLIENTS' EXPECTATIONS EARLY

1. Paul Jarvis, "The Importance of Settnig Client Expectations in 3 Steps," https://www.inc.com/paul-jarvis/the-importance-of-setting-client-expectations-in-3-steps.html.
2. Blair Thomas, "12 Tips about Managing Client Expectations You Can't Afford to Miss," https://smallbiztrends.com/2018/03/managing-new-client-expectations.html.
3. Tripp Watson, "What to Expect Working with Me," https://trippwatson.com/about-the-watson-firm/working-with-us.
4. Daniel Lazarz, "10 Ways to Set Clear Expectations with a New Client," https://www.forbes.com/sites/forbesagencycouncil/2018/03/25/10-ways-to-set-clear-expectations-with-a-new-client/#d50a3f87bef6.
5. Douglas Baldasare, "12 Tips about Managing Client Expectations You Can't Afford to Miss," https://smallbiztrends.com/2018/03/managing-new-client-expectations.html.
6. Twila Grissom, "10 Ways to Set Clear Expectations with a New Client," https://www.forbes.com/sites/forbesagencycouncil/2018/03/25/10-ways-to-set-clear-expectations-with-a-new-client/#d50a3f87bef6.
7. Angela Ruth, "12 Tips about Managing Client Expectations You Can't Afford to Miss," https://smallbiztrends.com/2018/03/managing-new-client-expectations.html.
8. Craig Klein, "10 Ways to Set Clear Expectations with a New Client,"

https://www.forbes.com/sites/forbesagencycouncil/2018/03/25/10-ways-to-set-clear-expectations-with-a-new-client/#d50a3f87bef6.

9. Ashley Hall, "4 Simple Rules to Manage Client Expectations," https://www.copper.com/blog/manage-client-expectations.

10. Ashley Hall, "4 Simple Rules to Manage Client Expectations," https://www.copper.com/blog/manage-client-expectations.

11. Linsey Knerl, "6 Ways to Level Up Your Business in 2019," https://www.nav.com/blog/6-ways-to-level-up-your-business-in-2019-33452/.

12. A sample and more thorough discussion of my litigation checklist spreadsheet is in my first book *Building a Better Law Practice*.

3.2.2 ESTABLISH YOUR PRIORITIES FOR CLIENT RELATIONSHIPS

1. Donald Miller, *Building a StoryBrand: Clarify Your Message so Customers Will Listen*, Kindle Loc. 2032.

3.2.4 YOUR CLIENTS HAVE CHOICES, BE THEIRS

1. "Disloyalty Is the New Black," *Nielsen*, https://www.nielsen.com/us/en/insights/article/2019/disloyalty-is-the-new-black/.

2. "Disloyalty Is the New Black," *Nielsen*, https://www.nielsen.com/us/en/insights/article/2019/disloyalty-is-the-new-black/.

3. Alyssa Gregory, "7 Ways to Take Your Small Business to the Next Level," https://www.thebalancesmb.com/small-business-next-level-2951535.

4. Micah Solomon, "The Four Secrets of Achieving Customer Satisfaction, *Forbes*, https://www.forbes.com/sites/micahsolomon/2018/06/10/the-four-elements-of-customer-satisfaction-how-to-achieve-it-over-and-over-again/#7a69f08528c2.